Praise for *Promoting Student Attention*

"Robin Wisniewski's refreshing new book helps educators reach out to the many students who may not have ADHD but still struggle with attention issues in the classroom. Her book is replete with the latest scientific findings on attention, evidence-based practices to help students better attend to their classroom work, rich teacher anecdotes, and 'Try This' experiments to help teachers learn more about the science of attention. You should definitely pay attention to this book!"

—**Thomas Armstrong, PhD**, author of *The Power of the Adolescent Brain* and *Neurodiversity in the Classroom*

"As the most connected yet disconnected generation, our youth face unprecedented attention challenges. Wisniewski offers practical, research-based strategies to help teachers foster focus and engagement in their classrooms."

—**Dr. José Manuel Villarreal**, principal, educational leader, futurist, coach, nonprofit board member

"Robin Wisniewski does a fantastic job of breaking down the science behind attention and focus for educators to better understand how the brain attends to stimuli and processes information. Furthermore, she does a thorough job explaining the tangible practices educators can implement in their classrooms to support all students' attention and engagement while keeping the whole child in mind."

—**Dr. Shane Saeed**, district ELA coordinator, author, and professional development facilitator/speaker

"Promoting Student Attention is a must-read for any teacher who's ever wondered: Why can't I get my students to pay attention? The answer, as Wisniewski describes with compassion for both harried teachers and distracted students, lies not in 'fixing' kids, but rather, in fixing *classrooms* to better reflect how kids' brains work. With clear and engaging prose, Robin Wisniewski demystifies the cognitive science of attention and then offers a plethora of classroom-tested, practical strategies teachers can use right away to grab and hold students' attention, redirect off-task behavior, and help students strengthen their ability to pay attention."

—**Bryan Goodwin**, president and CEO of McREL
International and lead author of *Learning That Sticks*
and *The New Classroom Instruction That Works*

"If you're searching for effective ways to engage unmotivated students, this book is a must-read. Its user-friendly tools and strategies guide you in identifying the root causes of problems before addressing solutions. The real-life stories of educators uncovering powerful methods to tackle off-task behaviors are truly inspiring."

—**Margaret Searle**, leadership and learning consultant for Searle
Enterprises and co-author of *Solving Academic and Behavior Problems*

PROMOTING STUDENT ATTENTION

PROMOTING STUDENT

How to Understand, Assess, and Create Conditions for Attention

ATTENTION

Robin Wisniewski

Arlington, Virginia USA

2800 Shirlington Road, Suite 1001 • Arlington, VA 22206 USA

Phone: 800-933-2723 or 703-578-9600

Website: www.ascd.org • Email: member@ascd.org

Author guidelines: www.ascd.org/write

Richard Culatta, *Chief Executive Officer;* Anthony Rebora, *Chief Content Officer;* Genny Ostertag, *Managing Director, Book Acquisitions & Editing;* Mary Beth Nielsen, *Director, Book Editing;* Liz Wegner, *Editor;* Beth Schlenoff, *Graphic Designer;* Valerie Younkin, *Senior Production Designer;* Kelly Marshall, *Production Manager;* Shajuan Martin, *E-Publishing Specialist;* Kathryn Oliver, *Creative Project Manager*

All web links in this book are correct as of the publication date below but may have become inactive or otherwise modified since that time. If you notice a deactivated or changed link, please email books@ascd.org with the words "Link Update" in the subject line. In your message, please specify the web link, the book title, and the page number on which the link appears.

PAPERBACK ISBN: 978-1-4166-3318-1   ASCD product #122014

PDF EBOOK ISBN: 978-1-4166-3319-8; see Books in Print for other formats.

Quantity discounts are available: email programteam@ascd.org or call 800-933-2723, ext. 5773, or 703-575-5773. For desk copies, go to www.ascd.org/deskcopy.

ASCD Member Book No. FY24-7 (Sep 2024 PSI+). ASCD Member Books mail to Premium (P), Select (S), and Institutional Plus (I+) members on this schedule: Jan, PSI+; Feb, P; Apr, PSI+; May, P; Jul, PSI+; Aug, P; Sep, PSI+; Nov, PSI+; Dec, P. For current details on membership, see www.ascd.org/membership.

Library of Congress Cataloging-in-Publication Data

Library of Congress Control Number: 2024030062

33 32 31 30 29 28 27 26 25 24   1 2 3 4 5 6 7 8 9 10 11 12

PROMOTING STUDENT ATTENTION

How to Understand, Assess,
and Create Conditions for Attention

Preface

During my first year of teaching developmental education, I noticed plenty of inattention in the class. One student had his head down on the desk. I finished my introduction to the concepts and provided the class with two steps to follow: write down the heading listed on each of the first three pages of the chapter we were going to read *before* they started reading it. As the other students began their work, I walked over to the student with his head on the desk, knelt down, and looked up at him. "Are you OK?" I asked. He looked at me with tired eyes and nodded. In a quiet voice, I continued: "What do you think about writing some headings down? I'll show you where we are in the book." He responded with a sleepy "OK." I opened his book and showed him the page. He took the book, put it on the table, and opened his notebook. "I'll come back and check on you," I said.

He sat up as he watched me walk away, glanced at the page, and then looked around at the students at his table to see what they were doing. He picked up his pen. I walked around to the other tables, modeled what to do, and told the class they had five more minutes to complete the task. I set my timer and walked back to kneel down again next to the student. He was in the right place in the book; I asked if I could show him what to do. He nodded, and I sat next to him, quietly talking aloud my thinking as I had done with several other students, reading the heading aloud, and writing it on his paper. He indicated he was ready to take over and write—and he did. After a few more minutes, I brought the class back together.

It was the first two weeks of classes, so I really didn't know this student well. There are always students who don't do the work, appear to daydream, have problems with the assignments, and talk to one another in class about personal matters. But this student started my experimentation. I introduced both small steps and the big picture, seeking to understand students and their perspectives and help them find their own strategies to regulate their learning, all while keeping a focus on the whole class. As I showed interest in his well-being and progress, I watched him increase his time on task.

First, Some Background

I am a student of psychology and education, holding undergraduate, master's, specialist, and doctoral degrees in these disciplines. I've learned a lot about learning as a teacher, psychologist, researcher, and human being by adopting multiple perspectives to construct and reconstruct knowledge.

So it's no surprise that this book takes a learning perspective. Its premise is that educators are learners who become better learners as we get better at teaching. Learning requires focus and attention, a seemingly straightforward prerequisite that, as all classroom teachers know, can be surprisingly complex. Maintaining students' attention in the classroom is essential, but it's also challenging and often frustrating to both teacher and student.

My developmental education students did not suddenly change their off-task behaviors. Quite the contrary. They struggled with reading, writing, and math. They escaped from work through daydreaming, wanted peer attention, wanted *my* attention, and were often distracted or tired. Most had experienced trauma, often racial and generational. These students wanted the same thing that we wanted when we were students: to be heard and to discover their own voices, identities, and learning pathways through life.

This classroom scenario took place in the 1990s, when interest in social cognition was on the rise. Donna M. Ogle's (1986) K-W-L chart—Know, Want to know, Learned—and Annemarie Sullivan Palincsar and Ann L. Brown's (1984) reciprocal teaching guided teachers in activating students' background knowledge and supporting questioning and predicting. These approaches also reflected how effective the teaching was and signaled changes teachers might make in the lesson going forward. They transformed into the "new literacies" of reading, writing, speaking, listening, and drawing, often deploying useful aids, such as graphic organizers and elaborate concept maps (Coiro et al., 2008). We focused on personalizing learning and differentiating the work for each student's strengths and challenges, building on their assets through culturally responsive teaching and curiosity through problem-based, project-based, and competency-based learning designs. These teaching and learning approaches permeate the approach to attention in this book.

I have since taught teacher education and leadership to both preservice and in-service teachers in universities and in short- and long-term professional development programs in schools. I've found that some teachers choose the profession because they want to replicate their student experience or because they love school, children, or their content area. Others teach to change the system and lift up students who need support or whose behaviors challenge adults. Many teach for a mix of these reasons. You know which one you are—you're the lover of learning, the system changer, the philosopher, the mathematician, the literary connoisseur, the artist, the coach, the student guide, the intellectual enthusiast.

I am the lover of learning. I enjoyed teaching adolescents and leading reading and counseling programs. As I gained experience, I built skills at guiding adults who teach, coach, and lead. I saw their strengths and struggles and wanted to support them so they could more fully enjoy the essence of good teaching. For me, this means lifelong learning for teachers and students alike as we continually work to improve education in a democracy.

About This Book

This book offers a process to use in your classroom with students who struggle with attention issues. Its purpose is to build a foundation for innovative thinking about this topic. Chapter 1 offers insights about attention, along with a framework for thinking about student attention. Chapter 2 describes how to assess inattention in the classroom and find root causes. Chapter 3 focuses on five principles for promoting attention, along with strategies to use right away. Chapter 4 looks at attention deficit hyperactivity disorder (ADHD), a special problem of attention. Chapter 5 discusses the experiences of several teachers I interviewed who created conditions for attention in their classrooms. Finally, in Chapter 6, I end with a call to action for improving student attention using strategies that are research-based, learner-centered, respectful—and, most of all, effective. Four chapters include special sections titled "Learn More," in which I discuss evolving neurobiology, related concepts and research, and additional areas in that chapter's topic area that readers might wish to explore.

So let's start this journey. By looking at attention in new and more productive ways, we can create an improved learning environment for all students in our classrooms.

Acknowledgments

Several people contributed to the start, continuation, and completion of this book. Genny Ostertag is the best coach I could ask for. Thank you to those who gave precise feedback: Yihua Hong, Natassia Rodriguez-Ott, and Mike Willoughby; advanced editors Merrie Aiken and Heather Hein; and Donna Fowler, who was the glue for the whole project. I'm grateful to Derek Grabski, Kersh Naidu, and Liza Selvarajah, who provided specific suggestions, especially for Chapters 2 and 4. I would also like to thank Ben Dalton, who provided unwavering opportunity, guidance, and support for significant improvements.

The following teachers also contributed to this book: Nycole Bradshaw, Marissa Coppock, Sandra Golden, Ash Hall, Adrienne Hayes, Venessa Kayrell, Seon Kim, Barbara Miller, Sean Miller, Liza Selvarajah, Danny Vuong, and Kevin Wilson. These thoughtful, innovative practitioners represent teachers of color in a book by another white female educator. They were gracious in lending their expertise not just in support of other teachers but to advance Black, Indigenous, Hispanic/Latine, Asian, and other people of color to the forefront of education discussions. These teachers also represent a range of grades, school types, and experiences across the United States. Thank you to those who recommended some of these teachers: Aime Black, Arnold Hillman, Masha Jones, Nardos King, Claudia Ladd, and Bess Scott.

My experiences were shaped by women who paved the way for my teaching and scholarship over the past 30 years: Debbie Shearer, Nancy Padak, Missy Gordon, and Karen Kaye. Over the past 12 years, Ceri Dean took me to new levels in education system improvement. Finally, and most important, I thank Judy Wisniewski, who enabled me to think as a learner, and L.A. Brandenburg, who supported me through the arduous process of completing a book.

Understanding Attention

Standing in front of the class, you turn toward the whiteboard to write down the main points of a lesson. Out of the corner of your eye, you see one student pick up their mobile phone and start texting. Another is whispering to a friend. When you turn back to the class, you see other students are looking around the room—and not at you.

You ask everyone to start a task, but then one student immediately asks you to repeat the directions. Another passes a note to a friend. Yet another has materials on their desk, but not the ones needed for the assignment.

A group of five students at a table watches you demonstrate a concept they will work on together or by themselves. The other students in the class are supposed to be working quietly as you demonstrate, but they're chatting about school or people they know.

Sound familiar?

These are some examples of student inattention in the classroom. As a teacher, you intuitively know that if students aren't paying attention, they aren't learning. And if they aren't learning, you may feel as though you're failing as a teacher. You've tried different strategies: redirecting, modeling on-task behaviors, using nonverbal cues, and offering incentives like extra points, but they don't seem to work. All students, to one degree or another, apparently have problems sitting still, following instructions, or staying on task.

Over the last quarter century, attention to attention has taken a turn. Not only are more students "not paying attention," a common teacher complaint, but inattention now is "so much worse." But this claim is unfounded. It's true that students today face more available distractions from social media, computers in their pockets and on their wrists, and ubiquitous connections to humans of all ages in all parts of the world. Yet attention has broader implications. We attend to what has meaning for us; our attention depends on conditions in our environment that enable or interfere with our ability to maintain focus. Distractions can disrupt attention, as can our intrusive thoughts related to the anxieties of day-to-day life.

Although I acknowledge the frustration behind many of the complaints about "kids these days," this book will not explain how to "fix" them. Indeed, I take the opposite approach. I focus on how to improve the adults in the classroom—ourselves.

We educators enable the next generation to think critically, solve life's problems, and participate responsibly in their communities. To do this successfully, we need to see ourselves as continually learning students, too. We're just more advanced and experienced students. We learn from all the people who surround us in our daily lives, including, and especially, the students in our classrooms. This book encourages teachers to pay attention to how they deal with inattention, to examine what inattention might mean for individual students, and to reflect on how changing their own approach to attention issues in the classroom can strengthen learning for all.

The Basics of Attention

What does it mean to "pay attention"?

When you're talking to a friend on the phone, you're paying attention. When students are engrossed in writing in a class, they are paying attention. When I am grading papers, I am paying attention. When students are playing a video game, they are paying attention. People pay attention when they talk, work, write, and play.

Attention is a cognitive process that enables us to attend actively to specific information in our environment while tuning out other details and stimuli. Attention includes the ability to switch our focus from one target to another and to maintain focus on a specific target for a sustained period of time.

We look at attention as an effect rather than a cause. This shift is important. Instead of seeing students' inattention as a problem *they* have, which can lead to ineffective criticism and judgment, we can become curious about *why* students may be inattentive and what we might do to address that. Truly understanding attention—its roots in cognition, the types of attention, and ways to think more constructively about it—enables teachers to take proactive steps to create better conditions for student learning.

To start, let's take a step back and look through a cognitive psychology lens to get a deeper understanding of how we learn and where attention fits in the learning process.

Attention and Cognitive Psychology

You are likely familiar with behavioral and cognitive psychology concepts from your educational psychology courses in college. Behaviorism was the dominant school of thought in psychology from the 1920s to the 1970s. It's hard to imagine now, but until the 1970s, psychologists believed that a student's mind was a "black box" too complex and inaccessible to understand or explain. For example, if we told a math student to write answers to problems on a piece of paper, what occurred in the student's mind (the black box) to figure out the problem was unobservable, so the focus was on what we could see—the student writing on the paper and producing a result. Behaviorists focused on reinforcement and punishment. If teachers wanted a student to complete a task, they offered positive reinforcement, such as giving students candy when the task was complete. To stop unacceptable student behavior, like leaving their seat, teachers would use negative reinforcements, such as taking away recess, or punishment, such as sending the student to the principal's office.

By the late 1960s, cognitive psychologists started changing how we think about thinking. They believed that what was going on in the black box was entirely relevant to learning and, therefore, worth figuring out. In 1968, University of California psychology professor Richard Atkinson and his student Richard Shiffrin developed a new model of cognition that outlined discrete steps in the thinking process. Influenced by the new field of cybernetics—a theory that each step, or action, in a system is an input for the next action—Atkinson and Shiffrin's model arranged the steps of cognition in a sequence of inputs and outputs.

With our math student in mind, consider Figure 1.1, which shows a series of inputs and outputs. The stimulus of telling the student to write answers to math problems is an input in the model. The student then goes through a series of thinking processes, or actions, to respond, from hearing the task directions, to working in small steps on the problem, to understanding and remembering the steps.

Figure 1.1 also labels the steps in the model. The student's thinking begins with information that enters through the senses, called *sensory memory* (the student hears and sees). Then the student maintains that information in their short-term memory, later dubbed *working memory*, which both stores a small amount of information for a short time and manipulates that information (the student works the math problem steps) (Baddeley & Hitch, 1974). Finally, the student processes that information so that it moves to *long-term memory* (the student understands and remembers the steps).

FIGURE 1.1

An Example of Inputs and Outputs Within the Information Processing Model

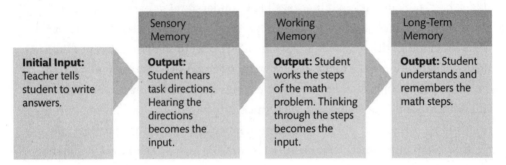

Try all three steps in the information processing model—those involved in sensory memory, working memory, and long-term memory—and see where attention fits. Imagine you are at a grocery store. When you walk down the cereal aisle, your eyes sense many items on the shelves, which you recognize as cereal boxes. You select a box, look at the ingredients, and note the grams of sugar and sodium. Then you turn to a different cereal and compare the contents to make a final selection. You notice that this box has an image of a bowl on the front, and you suddenly recall a visit you made to your grandmother, who had that cereal at her house.

What steps in the information processing model did you use? You sensed items, attended to one cereal box, kept information from the ingredients listed on that box in your working memory, and then went to the next box to compare ingredients. Then you made a decision, and some of the information from your decision-making process moved to long-term memory, whereas other information was forgotten.

The working memory manipulation could not have happened without attention. Attention kicks in right after receiving the information through our senses and before it shifts to our working memory. As we keep our attention on the cereal box, our working memory has time to manipulate the information.

Some of that information will then transfer to long-term memory (see Figure 1.2).

FIGURE 1.2

An Example of Attention Within the Information Processing Model

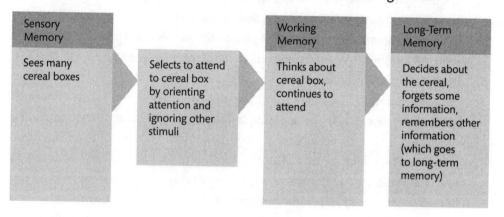

By understanding how attention fits into the steps of the information processing model, we can see that attention is essential in cognition—and that without attention, cognition stalls.

This information processing model sparked what is considered the *cognitive revolution*, the formal recognition of the study of cognitive psychology and the importance of thinking processes (Malmberg et al., 2019). This model has dominated research in the field of psychology for the last 50 years and is a basis for advances in the evolving neurobiology of attention (see "Learn More" at the end of this chapter). For our purposes, it is helpful to think of attention *as the step between sensation and working memory*.

Three Types of Attention

William James, who wrote the first known psychology textbook in 1890, illustrated the concept of attention this way:

> Everyone knows what attention is. It is taking possession of the mind, in clear and vivid form, of one out of what seems several simultaneously possible objects or trains of thought.... It implies withdrawal from some things in order to effectively deal with others. (pp. 403–404)

James says we intuitively know what attention is, yet he also points out its complexity. Even now, cognitive scientists continue to debate the concept of attention, and much still evades their understanding.

There are multiple types of attention (Pashler, 1997; Petersen & Posner, 2012; Posner & Petersen, 1990; Posner et al., 1988; Sohlberg & Mateer, 1989). To explore these types, consider your attention right now. As you are reading these words, many sensations around you might be claiming your attention. You may hear the hum of the traffic outside, feel the socks on your feet, or smell the dog bone you gave to your pup so that you could have some undisturbed time to read. As I point these sensations out, you organize the sensations and begin to actively pay attention to them.

This example illustrates the three attention types. You might choose to attend to your socks, while deciding to ignore conflicting sensory inputs, like the sound of the air conditioner. Then you might choose to disengage your attention from your socks and shift attention to look at the bone your dog is chewing. Then you might notice that your dog looks pretty cute holding the bone in her teeth, so you might sustain your attention for a time on her.

So attention is not as simple as "I am paying attention" or "the student is paying attention." These statements imply that we think of attention like a camera focusing on a singular object. Attention is much more complex. Rather, think of attention as consisting of the multiple ways that a camera focuses on objects: selecting an image and ignoring other images around it, moving the lens to a new scene, sharpening or blurring the background, and using a flash to take a picture.

Like this active and varied use of a camera, we use three main types of attention to focus on information:

- Selective attention
- Alternating attention
- Sustained attention

Let's look at these in more detail.

Selective Attention

Selective attention, the most familiar and studied type, is the ability to focus on the task at hand while rejecting other sensory input (Broadbent, 1958; Treisman, 1964). The classroom contains many sensory inputs making claims on student attention. Consider what you filter out while helping one student in your classroom with a writing task: papers rustling, students talking, chairs squeaking, the heater clunking, feet tapping, clocks ticking, mobile devices beeping. Your students, whose brains are not fully developed, also need to ignore these sensory inputs while selecting to focus on their individual writing tasks.

To understand selective attention, it is helpful to review the research process that cognitive psychologists use in the laboratory with both adults and children. A popular experiment is the *dichotic listening task*, where the subject wears headphones and is given the task of attending to sounds in one ear while filtering out sounds in the other ear (Moray, 1959). For example, researchers might instruct a subject to listen to a story in the left ear and ignore the story in the right ear. When the stories end, the subject is asked to repeat what they heard in each ear. Although they can recall sounds in the right ear, the subject can't repeat the story; the only story they recall is the one they heard in the left ear. This shows that someone can selectively attend to, or focus on, chosen stimuli in the presence of other distracting stimuli.

Researchers discuss selective attention as top-down (i.e., goal-directed) or bottom-up (i.e., stimulus-directed). The subjects in this experiment had a *goal-directed selective attention task*: to attend to the story in their left ear and ignore the story in their right ear. If, however, they heard a louder sound in their right ear and turned their attention toward it, this would be a *stimulus-directed selective attention task*. In the classroom, we want to see selective attention that is goal-directed and voluntary, where the student has control over selecting the target and rejecting the stimulus (Gazzaley & D'Esposito, 2007).

Selective attention is important from an early age. Toddlers would not learn to talk if they could not ignore a barking dog and traffic outside a window; they may hear sounds around them, but they ignore them to attend to the caregiver commanding their attention with a favorite toy. As the child develops, selective attention evolves from more stimulus-directed to more goal-directed and voluntary. This enables the child to deal effectively with all the sensory information in the environment, as well as with thoughts that could be troublesome, such as fear related to anxiety or recurring negative images related to depression (Posner et al., 2019).

By 7 years of age, a child has developed goal-directed selective attention skills (Rueda, Fan et al., 2004). In school activities, selective attention is essential in all tasks, from initiating assignments to focusing on a response, as opposed to just responding impulsively. Strategies for promoting selective attention can range from decreasing the amount of stimuli (Lavie et al., 2004) to helping the child set and carry out goals (Bradley et al., 2003; Pereira et al.,

2021). Moreover, when students have background knowledge of the target of attention, they are more likely to choose to attend to it (Awh et al., 2012).

Selective attention also is enhanced by what researchers call "reward history." For example, students may first choose to read a story with pictures of families like their own. As a result, they may experience satisfaction (the reward) from the story—confidence in their reading, positive feelings about the story—and so they may continue to choose to attend to reading.

> ### ✔ Try This: A Dichotic Listening Task
>
> Experiment with being a research subject by putting headphones on and listening to this video by OK Science on YouTube, "What Is Dichotic Listening and Selective Attention?" (www.youtube.com/watch?v=h-tQgfm2CAs). Focus on what you are hearing in one ear, and ignore the sounds in the other ear. What do you recall in your left ear? In your right ear? What was this experience like for you?

Alternating Attention

Alternating attention, also called *orienting,* involves three mental operations: disengaging one of our senses, like sight, from one activity or stimulus; moving to another stimulus; and then engaging with a new sense or object (Posner & Petersen, 1990; Sohlberg & Mateer, 1989). Let's say you are sitting at your desk, looking at your mobile phone. Your principal walks into the room to stand in front of your desk. First, you disengage your current focus on the phone. Second, you move your eyes to the new selected target, the principal. Last, you reengage your focus on the selected target, the principal.

Now, consider students alternating their attention when you ask them to move from one task to another. For example, a common task shift in elementary school is lining up in the classroom to leave. A student shifts from looking at a friend to look at the line, then looks back to the materials on the desk; puts away the materials; and, finally, gets up to join the line.

As with selective attention, cognitive psychologists have also researched alternating attention. The *cueing task* (Posner, 1980) examines how an individual performs an attention shift. Study participants are told to focus on an X at eye level on a computer screen. There is a box to the left of the X and a box to the right of the X. The researcher asks the participant to select the box where a dot appears. The researcher presents a cue *before* the dot appears, such as a horizontal line in the box. The cue consistently leads the subject's attention to move from one location to the target location.

The result shows not only the three steps in a shift (disengage, shift, and reengage), but also that this shift happens mentally *before* we move our eyes to the new target. The cueing task demonstrates this mind shift because the time delay between the cue and the dot is measured at just 100 milliseconds. This is insufficient time for the eyes to move to the dot, suggesting that the mind shifts before the eyes. The cue, therefore, not only leads to a shift in visual attention but also triggers the mind to attend to this shift beforehand.

This mental shift is called *covert orienting*, where we switch toward a new stimulus mentally, before our eyes or other senses move toward the new target. With *overt orienting*, our senses move right away.

In our daily lives, altering attention in the mind first is necessary. What would happen if we were in a grocery store aisle, looking at cereals to buy, and the fire alarm went off? We need to be able to disengage visually from looking at the cereal and reengage visually with the aisle so that we can get out of the store. The quicker we shift our mind first, the quicker we escape from danger.

Like selective attention, alternating attention can be directed by a stimulus, such as a fire alarm, but it is also voluntary, such as when choosing to reorient attention back to a task. Voluntary orienting can help children not only engage in a task but also disengage from intrusive thoughts or something fearful from a prior trauma. For example, if we've been in a fire previously and then see one in the grocery store, we may have difficulty quickly disengaging to look for the escape route (Posner et al., 2019).

Babies can reorient their attention in their first few months, and the voluntary shift of attention develops throughout childhood (Rothbart & Posner, 2015). In everyday activities, attention shifting is central to cognitive tasks. Students continually need to switch verbal and auditory attention from listening to a teacher or a peer, to reading or writing, to watching a demonstration. Cuing, as in the laboratory experiment, helps with orienting. If a teacher shows a certain image related to a topic, it can help learners switch attention to that topic. Also, when students have a positive relationship with a goal or the target stimulus, such as with a given task or a certain teacher, shifting attention toward that stimulus and away from other activities is easier.

When we selectively attend or reorient our attention, our attention focuses on a new stimulus: the book to read, the person giving instructions, the place to go to line up. The goal becomes *keeping* that focus, and that is where sustained attention—the third attention type we'll discuss—becomes important.

> ### ✓ Try This: A Cueing Task
>
> You may want to experiment by trying Posner's Cueing Task from psychological testing software provider Millisecond. Be sure to have about 15 minutes to complete the task. Go to www.millisecond.com/download/library/v6/cueingtask/cueingtask/cueingtask.web, follow the quick steps to download the demo, and click "start." What was this experience like for you—first of all, with the flashing boxes before the star appeared, and second, with the flashing arrows before the star appeared? Did you notice the mind shift before the visual shift?

Sustained Attention

Sustained attention is the ability to obtain and maintain an alert state, or focus, for an extended period of time (Fortenbaugh et al., 2017; Posner & Rothbart, 2018); we can consider it a combination of vigilance and concentration (Sohlberg & Mateer, 1989). In the classroom, you probably sustain your attention to students as you watch their behaviors to see if they understand a task or need help. Likewise, your students sustain their attention when they ask you questions and get feedback on their task. Selective attention is about ignoring interferences, whether those interferences are intrusive thoughts or peers talking in the corner, whereas sustained attention is the focus that occurs *after* that selection: you work on a task, you try different approaches, you go back to the beginning to check steps.

Researchers have studied sustained attention using experiments, such as *tests of continuous performance*, which examine how an individual focuses on a rarely occurring target on a computer screen while other, continually changing stimuli occur (Kim et al., 2015). For example, participants are asked to watch for the numbers 1 or 2 on a screen. If they see number 1, then they should click the mouse. But if they see number 2, they should not click the mouse. The challenge while watching is that attention may drift; in that case, the participant may not always click the mouse when number 1 appears or may inadvertently click it when number 2 appears. The more correct clicks, the more the individual displays sustained attention.

Tests of continuous performance mirror real-life situations where errors can occur during sustained focus. Air traffic controllers must continually watch for specific stimuli on radar. Truck drivers, airport security screeners, and soccer goalkeepers must also maintain sustained focus. Like inadvertently clicking on the mouse when the number 2 is present, a goalkeeper can err by moving to block the soccer ball when it appears to be flying into the goal but is really on a different trajectory.

Sustained attention develops throughout childhood, and some research shows rapid growth of this kind of attention between 5 and 6 years old and again between 11 and 12 years old (Betts et al., 2006). Although sustained attention is important in reducing errors in jobs and sports, it also has a great effect on learning. For example, when students sustain their focus on a math problem, text, or verbal presentation, they can hold that information in working memory so that learning—processing information into long-term memory—can occur.

Several factors influence students' sustained attention (Oken et al., 2006). When students are interested or the task has meaning for them, they are more likely to concentrate on it. But when they experience stress, focused attention may become difficult, and they may become hypervigilant to external sensations perceived as negative or as a threat. For example, a student with a negative relationship with the teacher may be hypervigilant about the teacher's location in the room, or a student encountering too much task information can lose focus due to the stress of not understanding. And, finally, when students maintain attention on a task over a long period of time, such as doing a repetitive computer task or too many math problems of the same difficulty level, their brains can start to see the constant stimulation as unimportant, causing a drop in focus (Ariga & Lleras, 2011). For this reason, laboratory studies of sustained attention offer participants breaks, as do real-life jobs requiring extended vigilance. After the events of 9/11, for example, airport security screeners started to get breaks every hour. This helped decrease errors in detecting potentially hazardous items on security X-ray screens. In the classroom, taking a break from focusing is a way to chunk the work; it gives students time to focus on one part of a task before starting another.

> ✓ **Try This: A Sustained Attention Response Task**
>
> Continuing in your role of research subject, try the Sustained Attention Response Task (SART) created by Robertson and colleagues (1997). Located at psytoolkit.org, this experiment calls on participants to hit the space bar in response to different numbers displayed on the computer screen, and then the demo catalogs your responses. What were your results? What was this experience like for you?

Putting Types of Attention into Context

In the real world, these three types of attention do not work independently. Rarely do we decide to attend to a target—and then nothing else happens. We might see a book on our nightstand and then pick it up and start reading it, using sustained attention. Or we might see the book on the nightstand, but then our spouse comes in the room and starts talking, and we alternate our attention to them. And sometimes we see a book, start reading it, and then stop to write down something from the book we want to remember. We are continually moving back and forth among the types of attention, with little or no awareness of the variation.

Similarly, students in the classroom are constantly solving mental conflicts, orienting their attention to new events, and focusing on new things throughout the day (Petersen & Posner, 2012). Modern attention research agrees: attention types are networked across brain structures using different brain chemicals, and some types also are combined and interact (Posner, 2023). Researchers continue to make new discoveries about how attention networks operate, even branching off into how attention connects with other cognitive processes documented over the years.

Knowing the basics of attention is essential to helping teachers understand that attention is a process and that conditions can be created to improve student attention. All three types of attention occur in the classroom all the time, and some strategies work best on discrete types of attention, while other strategies work on all three together. For example, chunking information helps with sustained attention, and when a student is presented with one small step of a task, they can then choose to attend to it or alternate their attention to it from a different activity.

We next explore how conditions in the classroom can influence this cognitive process. In other words, what happens when we think of attention as an effect rather than a cause?

Attention as Effect

Attention can be both a cause and an effect, depending on your vantage point. Consider a children's story in which the main character, a child, runs away, making their parents sad. Later we find out why the child ran away—to retrieve a teddy bear that a neighbor took the day before. The act of running away had a cause, just as the resulting act caused the parents' sadness.

We often think of attention as a cause in school. We may believe that focused attention or lack of attention causes students to persist or drop out of school or display high or low academic achievement (Arnold et al., 2020; Cortés Pascual et al., 2019). However, considering attention as an *effect* enables us to focus on understanding its causes and creating conditions for student-centered learning.

Think back to the information processing model in which sensory inputs preceded attention. We now know that attention not only is activated by our environment through our senses, but also is internal and voluntary, based on our experiences. Background knowledge, internal states, and ongoing needs are all causes of attention (Krauzlis et al., 2014). Figure 1.3 illustrates that these three areas, along with sensory input, are all attention activators.

FIGURE 1.3
Attention Activators

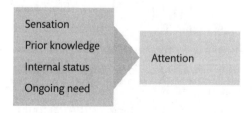

Let's think about how reframing attention as an effect of multiple causes can shift our understanding. Which statement—A or B—suggests you have control over your attention?

A. I was paying attention; therefore, I completed grading student papers.
B. I placed my distracting mobile phone out of reach; therefore, I was able to focus on grading student papers.

Sentence A describes your attention as something you just have or do, without recognizing what facilitated that attention in the first place. In sentence B, attention is *the effect of your putting your phone out of reach*. If you selected B, you saw your attention as an action you needed to take to complete your task. It assumes that attention is attainable—and that it can happen when we create the right conditions.

Reframing Attention as an Effect in School

If you've ever thought of a student as being lazy or indifferent about academics, you're not alone. If a student is consistently off task, it can be natural to attribute that behavior to the person's character (i.e., "This student just doesn't care about school"). This is known as the *fundamental attribution error* (Ross, 1977), where we overemphasize a person's character in evaluating a "bad" behavior and we underemphasize the situation. But if we were off task ourselves, we would attribute our behavior to the environment, like the content not being interesting—not our own character flaw.

As you can imagine, cognitive biases like the fundamental attribution error do not support student learning. If a teacher thinks students do not care about academics, the students may start to develop negative relationships with the teacher and engage in off-task behaviors or feel excluded, when all they needed was a little help with their learning.

Another common bias is *affinity bias*, our tendency to be drawn to people like us. Research on prospective teachers showed that if teachers were intrinsically motivated to perform, they tended to believe that students with on-task academic behaviors were similarly motivated and that students with off-task behaviors were lazy. The opposite was also true. Teachers who had avoided tasks in school didn't see off-task students as lazy, but, instead, viewed the students as lacking confidence or needing support in their work (Beghetto, 2007).

We are also not immune to racial bias. In a study of nationally representative samples of teachers over three decades, Bobo and colleagues (2012) found that compared to Black and Hispanic teachers, white teachers were more likely to rate Black and Hispanic students as "lazy" and to rate white and Asian students as "hardworking." (See Quinn & Stewart [2019] for a representative sample of teachers from 1975 to 2016.) It's important to note that compared with adults outside school, teachers have more positive perceptions of Black and Hispanic students (Quinn, 2017). This may be attributed, in part, to teachers' education levels because those with higher educational attainment generally have fewer implicit racial biases than those with lower attainment (Wodtke, 2012).

Our intentions, of course, are the opposite of these scenarios. We are committed to our students, so much so that such biases, despite being quite common, are difficult to admit, even to ourselves. Recognizing that we encounter stereotypical messages in the media and in our communities—and that these messages affect our social interactions—can help us turn around these biases in ourselves and others (Greenwald et al., 2002). If we don't recognize our own biases, we may continue to see attention as an effect of character. When students aren't paying attention, we may assume that something is wrong with *them*, that they're simply inattentive. This may prevent us from looking for the real cause.

Conclusion

This book doesn't just focus on simple reflections, like wondering about choosing cereal boxes or grading student papers. Instead, it invites us to engage in *critical reflection*, to become aware of and then question our own experiences and behaviors (Brookfield, 1995, 2017; Dewey, 1933). By doing so, we can more easily reframe our thoughts and attitudes and try new approaches.

Critical reflection can encourage more positive attitudes about students, which are linked to higher expectations and student achievement (Howard, 2003; López, 2017; Seriki & Brown, 2017). Such positivity is needed because decades of research tell us that teachers consistently attribute student academic or behavioral difficulties to the students themselves or to their families, instead of seeing these challenges as related to their own teaching or other factors (Wang & Hall, 2018).

Let's now put our critical reflection into play—along with our curiosity—and see how we can create the optimum conditions for attention.

Chapter Reflection: Rate Your Ability

This chapter introduced three types of attention. *Selective attention* is the ability to focus on the task at hand while rejecting other sensory input. *Alternating attention* is disengaging one of our senses from one activity or stimulus, moving to another stimulus, and then engaging with a new sense or object. *Sustained attention* is the ability to obtain and maintain an alert state or focus for an extended period of time.

First, rate your ability as 1, 2, 3, 4, or 5, with 5 being highest.

1. How would you rate your ability to select attention in the context of competing demands: 1, 2, 3, 4, or 5? Why did you select that rating?
2. How would you rate your ability to alternate your attention from one subset of possible sensory inputs to another: 1, 2, 3, 4, or 5? Why did you select that rating?
3. How would you rate your ability to sustain attention over long periods: 1, 2, 3, 4, or 5? Why did you select that rating?

Now that you have thought about your own attention, the next time you see a student who is on task, consider their attention as an effect, and ask yourself what is causing their attention. Consider this situation in the context of selective, alternating, and sustained attention. What might be interfering with the student's attention?

Learn More: The Complexities of Attention

The multiple types of attention presented in Chapter 1 derive from the information processing model, a dominant theory of cognition for the past 50 years. The concepts of selective, alternating, and sustained attention are based on experimental research in cognitive psychology, on clinical applications, and on an examination of the relationship of the three attention types in creating conditions for attention.

Since the late 1980s, researchers from the fields of cognition and neuropsychology have published descriptions of attention connected to brain structures and brain chemicals; these latter are referred to as *brain networks of attention* (Posner et al., 2016). These networks combine activating attention, focusing on a stimulus, and controlling attention; they're central to the neurobiology of attention. Leading the way in studying brain networks of attention, Posner acknowledges their incompleteness and expects that future research will "change" and "widen" these conceptualizations (Posner & Rothbart, 2023, p. 5).

Outside the main attention research community, other concepts of attention have emerged and become popular, such as the concept of *flow*. First described by Mihaly Csikszentmihalyi (1979, 2013), flow is an intense focus in a set of optimal conditions. These conditions include having interest, sufficient challenge, and goals to work toward, as well as getting immediate feedback in the task. Attention researchers have related flow to *hyperfocus*, "a phenomenon that reflects one's complete absorption in a task, to a point where a person appears to completely ignore or 'tune out' everything else" (Ashinoff & Abu-Akel, 2021, p. 1). Other researchers have focused on the concepts of internal and external attention (Chun et al., 2011), with internal attention based on thoughts and memory and external attention based on sensory information.

These are areas to explore in your ongoing learning about attention. In their treatise, "No One Knows What Attention Is," Hommel and colleagues (2019) describe such conceptual confusions as viewing attention as cause and effect, as well as the challenges associated with traditional methods of studying attention. They propose studying attention as an approach that integrates human cognitive, sensory, and behavioral processes.

2

Assessing Attention

A high school social studies teacher stands in front of the class and presents the guiding question for the new unit: "What is the meaning of civic participation in a democratic republic?" After explaining how the class will engage in civil discourse during the first lesson, the teacher expects students to observe, take notes, and ask questions.

In another school, a 1st grade teacher tells pairs of students to use letter blocks to form new words in the "am" word family. After giving the instructions, the teacher expects students to start moving their blocks around and talk with their partners.

In a 7th grade science class, the teacher directs students to get into their assigned small groups and use a graphic organizer to document the process of cell division. This teacher expects students to use their notes, help one another, and fill in their graphic organizers.

All three teachers have an expectation of what "attention" is for the task: students will be looking, doing, talking, and listening. But not all students will be on task. In the high school social studies class, some students draw, have their heads down, or whisper to peers. In the 1st grade classroom, one student gets up to walk toward the teacher, another runs around the room, and others play with various items on their table instead of working with the letter blocks. And in the 7th grade science class, some students are looking around the room, staring into space, and talking to friends about topics other than cell division. You probably see these off-task behaviors regularly.

Classroom researchers use on-task and off-task behaviors to assess attention (Godwin et al., 2013, 2016) because we cannot directly observe attention, only behaviors related to it. In other words, we cannot directly see if students are *selecting to attend* by blocking out distractions, *alternating attention* by moving their minds from the distraction back to the task, or *sustaining their focus* on the task. We can, however, observe *behaviors* and make inferences about what they mean for attention.

In this chapter, we focus on behaviors—on observing them and trying to understand why they occur. Specifically, we focus on behaviors considered to be off task. These range from the obvious, such as students leaving their seats, entering the classroom late, talking to peers, or throwing paper across the room, to the more subtle, such as students looking around the room or staring into space (Gill & Remedios, 2013). We first focus on individual students. This will help us see whole-class inattention patterns.

Five Principles for Assessing Attention

If you and I are sitting in the teachers' lounge, engaged in a face-to-face conversation, how do I know if you are paying attention to what I'm saying? You may be looking at me and listening to me talk about what I had for breakfast, but then your mind wanders to a task you need to complete. Or you hear other teachers talking by the coffee pot, and you tune into their voices instead. Perhaps you have no interest in what I had for breakfast, or you were politely waiting until I finished so you could get on with your day.

Suddenly, I notice you're looking at the teachers at the coffee pot. Then you move in your seat, and it looks like you're getting up.

"Hey! Pay attention to me!" I exclaim. "And sit back down!"

Your reaction? Shock, certainly, and annoyance. You might just stand up and disgustedly leave the lounge.

These *are* shocking demands coming from a colleague, but they are a common response among teachers to students who are off task. "Get back to work!" or "Sit back down!" are often our first responses to inattention in the classroom. They do little to encourage attention or stop off-task behavior. Not surprisingly, they can both impair the student–teacher relationship and foster negative teacher attitudes (Sugai & Horner, 2009).

As I tell you about my breakfast and then issue commands, my goal for you seems to be *obedience*. But you are an autonomous adult, and my goal instead should be to connect with you as a person. It's the same with our students. The more controlling we are, the less we support students in exercising their autonomy and the more negative their relationship with us becomes. Even a comment like "I need you to pay attention" sets up the conditions of teacher control and student obedience.

Our goal in assessing behavior is *not* to make students more obedient. Instead, it is to understand what's behind problematic behavior—that is, to learn more about individual students and their lives. The guiding question in this chapter is, Why is the student off task?

The following five principles can guide you in assessing attention.

Assessment Principle 1: Assess Individuals First

If you were a tutor, an academic coach, or an intervention specialist before teaching in a classroom, you might prioritize individual interactions with students or with small groups, as opposed to dealing with an entire class. On the other hand, if you started with whole-class teaching, you might prioritize whole-class interactions. Both perspectives are essential in the classroom, but focusing first on individuals can benefit the whole class.

Assessing individuals first establishes the basis for a whole-class attention perspective. Once you learn to identify, observe, hypothesize, and find root causes of individual obvious and subtle off-task behaviors, then you'll start to see classroom patterns. You can use these patterns to create conditions for attention and for continuous improvement of those conditions.

Assessment Principle 2: Be Flexible When Defining On-Task Behavior

In my breakfast discussion example, my expectation for your on-task behavior was that you sit, feet on the floor, arms folded on the table, and look at me until I finish talking. This is not a flexible definition of attention for you, your students, or me.

We define on-task behavior as the flexible range of behaviors demonstrating that students are engaged in a task. Students might be involved in their work, but doodle at the same time; they might be looking at and listening to the teacher, but intermittently chat with another student; they might be whispering with their peers, but then reengage in individual or paired work. However, these "flexible" behaviors do not always signify that students are on task (i.e., some people can doodle or chat with a peer while they listen, and some people can't).

Looking at on-task behavior in this more flexible way enables us to notice the ways students sustain their attention and how they alternate their attention to and from off-task behaviors.

Assessment Principle 3: Differentiate Types of Off-Task Behaviors

When I was telling you about my breakfast, you engaged in two types of off-task behaviors. The first one was obvious: you were getting up out of your seat. The second was more subtle: you were looking at the teachers near the coffee pot. I was not sure if you were listening to me, and I may not have even noticed if you were alternating your gaze between the teachers and me.

In the classroom, the teacher notices the obvious off-task behaviors, like students leaving their seats, which can potentially interfere with other students' attention. In contrast, a teacher may or may not notice more subtle off-task behaviors, such as students looking around the room. They could be daydreaming, but they're not interfering with other students.

It helps to differentiate between obvious and subtle behavior. First, when we look at a classroom of students who are off task and we don't understand why, we can easily become frustrated. Focusing on individual behaviors helps us discover the causes, which leads to change. Second, it's easier to notice a behavior that interferes with others' progress. When we label this obvious behavior, we're less likely to react to it and more likely to investigate why it's occurring. Finally, labeling subtle behaviors calls our attention to students whose behavior is *not* disruptive, to students we may fail to notice. It encourages us to promote conditions of attention for all our students.

✔ Try This: Defining Behaviors

Experiment with your own definition of on-task and off-task behaviors. Choose a lesson that you commonly conduct with your students.

- Do a quick-write of behaviors you expect to see as you introduce, facilitate, or conclude the lesson.

- Review your list while considering the second assessment principle ("Be flexible when defining on-task behavior"). Have you included a flexible range of behaviors, such as students drawing, looking at the teacher while talking with peers, or whispering during individual or paired work?

- Observe students during your lesson. What do you notice about their on-task behaviors? What do you notice about potential off-task behaviors? Consider the third assessment principle ("Differentiate types of off-task behaviors").

Assessment Principle 4: Seek the Why

In the teachers' lounge, I had exclaimed, "Hey, pay attention to me!" when I saw you move to stand up. My reaction was not just shocking. It was also a direct response to your obvious off-task behavior. What I neglected to do was try to understand *why*. Was the chair uncomfortable? Were you escaping from me? Did you want someone else's attention? Were you getting up to get coffee?

These questions reflect four possible immediate reasons for off-task behaviors based on functional behavior analysis (FBA). Other reasons are derived from attention research: (1) you were distracted by an unrelated sound (the coffee pot fell); (2) you were interrupted by a related sound (someone else talking about breakfast); (3) you were interrupted by an unrelated thought (what you'll do in your classroom today); or (4) you were interrupted by a related thought (what you had for breakfast).

These immediate reasons, either based on functional behavior analysis or from attention research, tell us why an obvious or subtle off-task behavior occurred. But they don't yet give us enough information to adjust conditions for attention. After this first "why," we must seek the underlying causes for the off-task behavior. We will get to the five root causes shortly. The root cause gets us closer to the assessment goal, which is to create conditions for attention.

Assessment Principle 5: Know the Assessment Goal

Creating conditions for attention is the opposite of what I did in the teachers' lounge when I raised my voice to get you to listen to me. I was trying to change you—and using punitive behaviors to do so. Research shows that punishment, such as yelling, requiring students to write sentences over and over, demanding students' attention, or isolating them because of their off-task behaviors, does not work. These punishments can reinforce the behavior they were intended to stop and damage both teacher–student relationships and students' capacity for self-regulation (Rothbart & Jones, 1998; Ryan & Deci, 2006).

Our assessment goal is not about fixing students. It is about taking what we understand about inattention and using it to improve what we do as teachers.

Why Off-Task Behaviors Occur: A Functional Behavior Perspective

In the 1980s, researchers wondered about children and adolescents who displayed self-injuring behavior in school. Up to this point, they found that isolating the student or removing a toy from a child who was self-harming by hitting, biting, or banging their head did not stop the behavior. In fact, punishment seemed to reinforce the behavior, causing continued self-harm. This led to a research question that focused on the cause: *Why* is the person hitting themself?

To find out, researchers set up three different environments for nine children and adolescents with self-injuring behavior (Iwata et al., 1982, 1994). In the "academic condition," the individual was presented with task demands by the experimenter. In the "alone condition," the individual was left alone in a room with no toy materials. And in the "attention condition," the individual was left in a room with both toy materials and the experimenter. In each environment, the individual received a different response when they started a self-injuring behavior: removal of the task demand in the academic condition; lack of a response in the alone condition (although the experimenter would intervene to stop the harmful behavior); and brief experimenter attention in the attention condition.

Researchers tested the individuals in random order for 15 minutes at a time. The experiment stopped for each individual as their responses became stable, or after 12 days of assessment. For example, when the individual's self-injuring behavior stopped consistently when task demands were removed in the academic condition, the researcher halted the experiment and labeled the reason for the behavior as "escape," or avoiding the task demand.

You may recognize these reasons for behavior if you have ever been involved with a functional behavior assessment (FBA) for a student in your school. An FBA assesses for one of the four "functions" of behavior, which I am describing as immediate reasons for behavior in this chapter. This study was so revolutionary that FBAs are now common in schools, from its methods of assessing reasons for behaviors, to its conclusion that there were three reasons for these self-injuring behaviors: to escape from a task, to get sensory stimulation, or to get attention from another person. These results were replicated in experiments over the next 40 years with behaviors like these, as well as with more aggressive behaviors (such as yelling or throwing items) and relatively minor off-task behaviors (such as laying one's head down on a table or not doing one's homework) (Bruni et al., 2017; Watson et al., 2001). The researchers ultimately added a fourth reason for off-task or negative behaviors: to get something tangible (e.g., a young child yelling to get a toy). Figure 2.1 defines each of these four reasons.

The study had another insightful conclusion: different people can display the same severe behavior, like hitting themselves, for completely different reasons.

This is also true in the classroom: a high school student may consistently walk in late to avoid the tasks at the beginning of class or to get attention from peers.

FIGURE 2.1

The Four FBA Reasons for Off-Task Behavior

Reasons	The Immediate Reason for the Student's Behavior Is...
Escape from task	To avoid, or escape from, the task.
Sensory stimulation	Because the behavior feels good or provides some sensory relief.
Attention seeking	To gain attention, either from adults (like the teacher) or from peers.
Tangible reward	To get something concrete (i.e., an object).

✔ **Try This: Four Reasons for Behavior**

You may want to experiment with your own behaviors to discover the reasons that behaviors occur from the functional behavior perspective. During the next 10 minutes, notice your physical behaviors. This may include getting up from your seat, walking across the room, or researching a topic on the internet. Choose one behavior and write it down. What was your initial reason for doing it? Were you getting up from your seat because it felt good (sensory stimulation)? To reach for a pencil (tangible reward)? To avoid reading more (escape from task)? How about walking across the room? Did you do so to get someone's attention (attention seeking)? Or to get your laptop (tangible reward)?

Applying a Four-Step Procedure to Obvious Off-Task Behavior Using the Functional Behavior Perspective

Unlike the research with self-harm behaviors, you won't be running experiments in your classroom. Instead, you can use four steps to discover which of these are immediate reasons for the behavior to get to the root cause for obvious off-task behaviors: (1) label the behavior; (2) observe the behavior; (3) hypothesize the cause as one of the above four research-based behavior reasons; and finally (4) dig deeper to find a root cause of the behavior. We'll walk through each step using an example of a common obvious off-task behavior: a student getting out of their seat (Nelson et al., 1998).

Step 1: Label the Off-Task Behavior

You may hear teachers say that a student is "disrespectful," "noncompliant," or "angry." None of these describes a behavior. The first two simply apply value judgments to the behavior, and the third describes an emotion. But behavior is an action that we can see or hear—getting out of a seat, throwing a chair, hitting, yelling, talking, or tapping a pen on a desk.

An obvious off-task behavior interferes with attention if it is *frequent* (talking to peers many times during an hour), of *sufficient duration* (laying one's head down on a table for five minutes at a time), or *intense* (yelling loudly). These behaviors diminish on-task time and disrupt the attention of peers and the teacher.

Let's look at the behavior of a student who gets up many times during a lesson. This takes away from on-task time, and it's obvious because it disrupts peer attention. We label the behavior "leaving the seat" so that we know what to observe.

Step 2: Observe the Behavior

We've labeled the behavior of leaving the seat. Now we observe. You may say, "I don't have time to observe!" You won't be conducting in-depth observations while teaching. Instead, the goal is to practice the following protocol so that you know what to look for and can observe more quickly over time.

There are two areas to observe: the *context* of the behavior and the *physical dimensions* of the behavior. The context is what surrounds the behavior—what occurs before the behavior (the antecedent) and after it (the consequence). This is called an ABC (antecedent-behavior-consequence) analysis.

Figure 2.2 is a typical observation protocol that includes the off-task behavior (fourth column), as well as an antecedent (third column) and a consequence (fifth column) each time the behavior occurs. In this example, the observation took 20 minutes. In a high school classroom, you might observe the behaviors over a single period or over multiple days; in an elementary class, you may see them throughout the day.

Let's look at the occurrences first. Notice how these columns describe the context without applying value judgments or speculating about the student's emotions.

During the observation, the first five occurrences consist of the student leaving their seat after the teacher gives a direction for independent work (e.g., write your name on the paper, complete the sentences). Teacher responses include telling the student to sit down; ignoring the behavior three times; and

FIGURE 2.2

ABC (Antecedent, Behavior, Consequence) Chart for Off-Task Behavior

Occurrence	Time	Antecedent (What happened before the behavior, such as what the teacher says, what is happening in the environment)	Behavior (Off-task behavior, along with incidents of on-task behavior)	Consequence (What were the results or reactions? What was said? What did peers or the teacher do?)
1	9:13	Teacher says, "Write your name on the paper."	Student gets up out of seat.	Teacher tells student to sit down. Student sits, then puts head down.
2	9:14	Teacher says, "Write these five words on your paper down the left side," then writes the five words on the board.	Student gets up out of seat.	Teacher does not react. Student stays out of seat until the task is complete.
3	9:16	Teacher says, "For the next five minutes, read pages 8–9 and circle these five words" and writes "pages 8–9" on the board.	Student gets up out of seat and walks to the back of the room.	Teacher does not react. Student stays out of seat until the task is complete.
4	9:20	Teacher says, "For the next 10 minutes, write sentences using the five words."	Student gets up out of seat.	Teacher does not react. Student wanders to the window, looks out, then sits back down as the teacher walks away.
5	9:21	Teacher walks to front of the room to write instructions on the board.	Student gets up out of seat.	Teacher walks over to student and says that if student gets up again, then student must go to principal's office. Student walks slowly to seat.
6	9:22	Teacher says, "Work with your table partner to check your sentences."	Student works on task beside table partner; student whispers.	Teacher notices but ignores the student.
7	9:28	Teacher asks student to stop talking and do their own work.	Student continues to work and whisper occasionally with table partner.	Teacher tells student to go to an independent work area at the back of the room to work alone.
8	9:33	Teacher tells student to finish the task they started and partially completed with the table partner.	Student gets up out of seat and sharpens pencil; does not return to independent work area.	Teacher sends student to principal's office.

warning the student that if they get up again, they will be sent to the principal's office.

Occurrence 6 is different. The student is on task, specifically after the teacher tells students to work with their table partners. But despite the on-task behavior, the teacher notices the student whispering and isolates the student from others. The problem behavior occurs again, and the teacher sends the student to the principal's office.

Now let's turn to the *physical dimensions* of the off-task behavior. These define the behavior in terms of its frequency (how often), duration (how long), and intensity (how strong). During this observation, the student gets out of their seat six times. The *duration* is how long the student is out of their seat; for example, "Student stays out of seat until the task is complete." The *intensity* is different: four times, the student gets out of the seat quickly and twice, more slowly.

You now know the formula and the details to look for. Over time, you will improve at deciphering the context and physical dimensions. This will enable you to more quickly hypothesize about the reasons for the behavior.

Step 3: Hypothesize the Cause

Now look at the sixth column in Figure 2.3, which adds the possible immediate reason for the behavior: escape from task, sensory stimulation, attention seeking, or tangible reward. Six off-task behaviors (occurrences 1–5 and 8) and two on-task behaviors (occurrences 6 and 7) are listed in the table.

The six off-task behaviors (getting out of the seat) have two possible reasons: to escape from the task or get attention from the teacher. Escape is listed because the student did not return to on-task behavior after the consequence. "Attention from teacher" is listed in two incidents because the student returned to their seat *only* after getting the teacher's attention. We can disregard other reasons for these six occurrences, such as attention seeking from peers (there were no peer reactions to the problem behavior), sensory stimulation (behaviors only occurred after a teacher task demand), or tangible reward (the student did not get anything tangible).

Here's a brief template for writing an overall hypothesis: When [event (antecedent)] occurs, the student engages in [off-task behavior], and then [what happens after the behavior (consequence)] occurs. Therefore, the most likely immediate reason for the student's behavior is [possible reason].

To create an overall hypothesis, let's review. In the six off-task behaviors, the teacher reacted in occurrences 1 and 5, but the student did not start the

FIGURE 2.3

ABC Chart, with Possible Reason Added

Occurrence	Time	Antecedent (What happened before the behavior, such as what the teacher says, what is happening in the environment)	Behavior (Off-task behavior, along with incidents of on-task behavior)	Consequence (What were the results or reactions? What was said? What did peers or the teacher do?)	Possible Reason (What was the payoff? Why might the behavior be happening?)
1	9:13	Teacher says, "Write your name on the paper."	Student gets up out of seat.	Teacher tells student to sit down. Student sits, then puts head down.	Attention seeking (from teacher)
2	9:14	Teacher says, "Write these five words on your paper down the left side," then writes the five words on the board.	Student gets up out of seat.	Teacher does not react. Student stays out of seat until the task is complete.	Escape from task
3	9:16	Teacher says, "For the next five minutes, read pages 8–9 and circle these five words" and writes "pages 8–9" on the board.	Student gets up out of seat and walks to the back of the room.	Teacher does not react. Student stays out of seat until the task is complete.	Escape from task
4	9:20	Teacher says, "For the next 10 minutes, write sentences using the five words."	Student gets up out of seat.	Teacher does not react. Student wanders to the window, looks out, then sits back down as the teacher walks away.	Escape from task
5	9:21	Teacher walks to front of the room to write instructions on the board.	Student gets up out of seat.	Teacher walks over to student and says that if student gets up again, then student must go to principal's office. Student walks slowly to seat.	Attention seeking (from teacher)

Occurrence	Time	Antecedent (What happened before the behavior, such as what the teacher says, what is happening in the environment)	Behavior (Off-task behavior, along with incidents of on-task behavior)	Consequence (What were the results or reactions? What was said? What did peers or the teacher do?)	Possible Reason (What was the payoff? Why might the behavior be happening?)
6	9:22	Teacher says, "Work with your table partner to check your sentences."	Student works on task beside table partner; student whispers.	Teacher notices but ignores the student.	Attention seeking (from peers)
7	9:28	Teacher asks student to stop talking and do their own work.	Student continues to work and whisper occasionally with table partner.	Teacher tells student to go to an independent work area at the back of the room to work alone.	Attention seeking (from peers)
8	9:33	Teacher tells student to finish the task that they started and partially completed with the table partner.	Student gets up out of seat and sharpens pencil; does not return to independent work area.	Teacher sends student to principal's office.	Escape from task

on-task behavior; they either put their head down or reluctantly returned to their seat. This suggests that attention from the teacher is not what the student needs because the student continued off-task behaviors. Similarly, in the on-task occurrences 6 and 7, the student is on task after the teacher directions, suggesting that they are not seeking teacher attention when the context changes to working with peers rather than alone.

Therefore, teacher attention is not a primary reason for the off-task behaviors. Writing the hypothesis using the ABC formula would look like this: When the teacher gives directions for the task, the student gets out of their seat and does not start the task. Therefore, the student's most likely immediate reason for the behavior is escape from the task.

Now that we've identified the student's target behavior and the most likely immediate reason for it, we're ready for the last step: finding the root cause of the off-task behavior.

Step 4: Find the Root Cause

Why is the student getting out of their seat? They are escaping the task. To find a solution for the initial inattention—the off-task behavior problem—we need to find a root cause for the student's motivation to escape tasks.

Five root causes are common reasons for off-task behaviors (Hofer, 2007; Kilian et al., 2010; Saripah & Widiastuti, 2019). The off-task behavior occurs because the student

- Does not know what to do or how to do it.
- Does not find the task meaningful, relevant, or interesting.
- Lacks a variety of ways to interact with the content.
- Does not feel a sense of belonging in the classroom.
- Lacks a sense of autonomy or capacity for self-monitoring.

We consider these root causes because by addressing any one of them, a teacher can promote greater attention. To determine the most likely root cause for a student's off-task behavior, we would also need to see that the problem behavior ceases if we remove the root cause.

A popular root cause analysis tool is the 5 Why strategy. The creator, who used it for addressing problems in car manufacturing, believed that asking "why" at least five times yielded a solution (Ohno, 1978, 1988). The number can be fewer than five if it gets you to the root cause. Here is an example of the process with four whys:

- Why is the student getting out of their seat? *Answer*: They are escaping the task.
- Why are they escaping the task? *Answer*: Because it does not interest them.
- Why are they not interested? *Answer*: The task has no meaning for them.
- Why does the task have no meaning for them? *Answer*: The teacher did not incorporate student background or interests into the task.

As you can see, this process ends with an answer that the teacher can address to improve the conditions for attention.

You may notice some limitations with the 5 Whys. The technique has been widely criticized because different people using it to analyze the same behavior can come up with a variety of root causes (Card, 2017). For example, the question of why a student seeks escape from a task can result in many reasons, such as not knowing what to do, having to deal with too much information, or finding the task irrelevant.

But we can make use of the most essential aspect of the 5 Whys: asking "why" until we get to a likely root cause, one we can address. In our example, the student is leaving their seat to avoid the task, but we still don't know why they are avoiding it.

Before asking why, consider student skills: does the student have the reading and writing skills needed for the task? In this example, the teacher has looked over summative assessment results from the previous academic year and has observed that the student has demonstrated these skills in her own formative assessments. So the teacher can rule out lack of skills.

It's challenging to get to a root cause without talking with the student. You might consider an interview or simply try to get to know them better. The following conversation asks directly about the event. You might start by getting the student's agreement for you to ask questions about the task, sharing why you are asking and using an interested, curious tone to invite them into an exploratory conversation.

> Teacher: Would you mind if I asked you some questions real quick about the lesson we just had? I'd like to explore what you think about the task.
>
> Student: It's OK.
>
> Teacher: It seems you may be avoiding the task you're supposed to do. Do you think that's true? Do you think you're avoiding the task? [Hypothesized reason for the target behavior]
>
> Student: Yeah, I guess.
>
> Teacher: Why do you think you're avoiding it?
>
> Student: I don't want to do it.
>
> Teacher: Why do you think you don't want to do it? [Probing questions might include, Is it just not interesting? Do you not know what to do with the task or how to do it?]
>
> Student: It's boring.

Figure 2.4 shows three examples of the 5 Whys and how they can lead to a different root cause. Notice how listening to the student can help you get to a more accurate reason. Just like any assessment, the more you do it, the better you get.

The first "why" question is the easiest because it's based on our hypothesis: why do we think the student is escaping? The answer "I don't want to do it"

FIGURE 2.4

Using the 5 Whys: Three Examples

Student gets out of seat	Student gets out of seat	Student gets out of seat
• Why? Task avoidance	• Why? Task avoidance	• Why? Task avoidance
• Why? Doesn't like the task	• Why? Doesn't like the task	• Why? I don't want to do it
• Why? There are better things to do	• Why? It's stupid	• Why? It takes too long
• Why? Other things are more fun, like talking to friends	• Why? It has nothing to do with me	• Why? I don't know; it's just too much to do
• Why? The work is boring	• Why? I don't know why; it has no relevance to my life	• **Root Cause** **Doesn't know what to do or how to do it**
• Why? Because it's just reading	• **Root Cause** **Doesn't find the task meaningful, relevant, or interesting**	
• **Root Cause** **Lacks a variety of ways to interact with the content**		

doesn't lead to a practical solution; we still cannot make a person *want* to do something. We need to know more about why they don't want to do it.

So we ask "why" again. Why does the student not want to do the task? They may tell us that they don't like it or that it's a lot of work. These answers might suggest that the root cause stems from there being too much information for the student to take in or because they simply don't understand what to do. But the student said, "It's boring."

"It's boring" is a common response from students. In fact, research shows that by the time students get to middle school, they cite tasks related to reading informational texts as dull, irrelevant, or arduous (Guthrie et al., 2012). Although "it's boring" is a mundane answer, it gives us useful information for a possible root cause and a baseline for asking further questions (e.g., when the student *is* on task, we can ask what they like about it or what they find interesting).

In the case of the student getting out of their seat, the teacher already observed this student being on task with other students (the student returned to being on task in occurrences 6 and 7, so we know they knew what to do and that being in a social context is what they needed to complete the task). So "boring" may signify that working by themselves is not enjoyable, leading us to consider a potential root cause—that the student may have just one static way of interacting with the content.

The next question should lead to the goal of developing a strategy for improved attention, such as asking the student if they like working alone or with others and in what circumstances. You can then try some peer work strategies (see Chapter 3) that align to the root cause. Trial-and-error is involved, too, as we test different solutions to determine which ones work and then adjust as we see increased attention.

The more we use the process, the more it becomes a routine way of thinking. As soon as we see an off-task behavior, we can identify it, describe how often it occurs, note what happened before and after the behavior, gather more data over time, hypothesize the reason, and then determine its root cause.

The behaviors discussed so far are obvious, and we examined them using the reasons provided from functional behavior research. In the next section, we use these steps to assess subtle off-task behaviors, such as gazing around the room. This time we examine the immediate reasons from a cognitive perspective using *attention interferences*.

Why Off-Task Behaviors Occur: A Cognitive Perspective Using Attention Interferences

You've been noticing that you have not been as attentive in your teaching as usual. When you listened to a student explaining some problem they had, you found yourself predicting what they would say, and then you tuned out, having heard all this before. As you drove home from work, you thought about what your students may have learned in school that day.

When you got home from school, you sat down to answer emails from parents and colleagues and, after you responded to one, an email popped up from that parent, so you responded directly. Then you heard a notification on your phone, picked it up, checked the app, and started scrolling. Thirty minutes passed. Tired now, you figured you would leave the rest of the emails for tomorrow.

In this scenario, we see several attention interferences that are internal, from within ourselves (tuning out), and external, from our environment (email notification) (Chun et al., 2011). For example, we might be working on emails to parents but also have internal interferences, such as feeling stress from an argument we had earlier in the day or thinking about what to make for dinner. We might be working on those emails but experience external interferences, such as hearing a text notification or seeing our cat walk across the computer keyboard. Figure 2.5 shows examples of these two interference sources.

FIGURE 2.5
Two Sources of Interference

Source of Interference	Example
Internal	• Recalling an argument you had earlier in the day • Walking into a room and forgetting why you went there • Thinking about what to make for dinner • Daydreaming while driving your car • Reflecting on your driving skills while driving your car • Thinking about another class while listening to a world history lecture
External	• A notification alert from your phone • Your cat walking across your keyboard while you type • Hearing your name mentioned from across the room • A new email arriving while you're reading an adjacent one • Messages popping up on the computer during your research

We can also break down these two sources of interference in terms of whether the subject is on topic or off topic (Keller et al., 2020). When on topic, we call these interferences *diversions* and *interruptions*; when off topic, we call them *intrusions* and *distractions* (see Figure 2.6).

FIGURE 2.6
Four Types of Attention Interferences

	Internal	External
On topic	Diversions	Interruptions
Off topic	Intrusions	Distractions

Let's look at these a little closer with some examples:

- You tuned out—you started to think about what the student would say—when they were talking to you about a problem. This is an internal interference that was on topic, a *diversion*.
- You started working on emails but turned to a related email that popped up. This is an external interference that was on topic, an *interruption*.
- You daydreamed while driving. This is an internal interference that was off topic, an *intrusion*.
- You responded to a mobile phone notification when you sat down to answer emails. This was an external interference that was off topic, a *distraction*.

Each of these behaviors is subtle. When our mind wanders or phone notifications occur, they interfere with our on-task behavior—and our attention—and we are suddenly, and subtly, off task. Our own subtle inattention can go unnoticed, just like our tendency to not notice a student's wandering gaze, as opposed to noticing a student getting up from their seat. A close look at subtle off-task behaviors can help us understand inattention; we can get to a root cause using a cognitive route, rather than the behavioral one we used for obvious behaviors.

✓ Try This: Types of Attention Interferences

Revisit the list of behaviors you jotted down when you read through the "Try This" section on the four functions of behavior (escape from task, sensory stimulation, attention seeking, tangible reward). If you didn't write any behaviors down, notice your behaviors in the next 10 minutes, and write those down.

Choose one that is more subtle, such as looking out the window or somewhere other than the page you're reading. Then answer these questions: What was the initial reason for this inattention, based on attention research? Did you look out the window because you started thinking about a student who is frequently off task in your classroom? This would be a *diversion* (internal on-topic). Or did you look somewhere else in the room because you remembered something you needed to be doing instead of reading this book (*intrusion*, internal off-topic)? Or did you look at your phone because there was a text notification (*distraction*, external off-topic)?

Applying the Four-Step Procedure to Subtle Off-Task Behavior Using the Cognitive Perspective

To recognize and assess these subtle behaviors and their interferences, we'll follow the same steps we used in our analysis of obvious off-task behaviors. This time we'll look at the common subtle off-task behavior of looking around the room and use the four attention interferences as immediate reasons for these subtle off-task behaviors.

Step 1: Label the Off-Task Behavior

Describe your behavior while you were listening to that student who was explaining a problem they had. For example, you may have shifted your eyes, stared into space, or even shifted your weight while standing or sitting. All of these are subtle, off-topic behaviors. It's more challenging to define these behaviors in our students because we must infer the reasons behind them; we can't observe a student's thoughts. This particular behavior—looking around the room—is a good example to use for proceeding through the next steps.

Step 2: Observe the Behavior

Teacher Venessa Kayrell tells the story of an 11th grade student in geometry class who used a calculator to find the area of a shape. The student started to write the answer—162 cm—starting with 1 and 6, then paused and looked around. He looked back to the paper and said, "Oh, yeah," and filled in the 2. After writing the 2, there was another pause and a look into the distance for a few moments. Then the student said, "Oh, I have to write the centimeters squared."

Familiar with the ABC analysis, Venessa observed the context of the behavior and what happened before the student began looking around (antecedent). The classroom had a wall of windows, and the student would become, according to Venessa, "fascinated with the gardeners outside," or he would watch the ball spinning on the table-top fountain on Venessa's desk. The student would watch this fountain frequently and at length, taking considerable time away from independent math tasks. After looking away, the student alternated his attention back to the task at hand.

Step 3: Hypothesize the Cause

Venessa hypothesized that most of this student's attention interferences were external and off topic. This pointed to *distraction* as the type of interference. Venessa tested her hypothesis by partially closing the window drapes, turning off the desk fountain, and slightly repositioning the student's chair. These changes seemed to work. The student's frequency of looking around the room decreased, and he seemed to take fewer pauses during the math problems. Distractions are probably the easiest of the four interferences to spot because there's something in the environment drawing the student's attention away.

Intrusions (internal off-topic interferences), on the other hand, can be more difficult to observe. In her 12th grade science class, Venessa noticed a student who had a wandering mind. She explained, "When we were talking, I could see her eyes zone out. I could see her go to another space, and she would come back, look at me finally, and say, 'Oh, could you repeat the question?'"

Venessa discovered that the antecedent to this mind wandering was when her teaching was "too word heavy." When the student alternated her attention back to her, Venessa learned to more succinctly focus solely on the next step in the task.

In both of these cases, the hypothesis for the students' subtle off-task behaviors pointed to off-topic interferences, either external (distractions) or internal (intrusions). But on-topic interferences—diversions and interruptions—don't have to be disruptive. They can be part of a good learning environment where peers work together and collaborate to create classroom rules.

Doodling is a common subtle off-task behavior, but some students may be listening *while* they doodle. Diversions may occur for those who doodle while listening or taking notes, but these on-topic interferences might be making connections to the topics in the notes. Or an interruption can occur when a student asks a question. The teacher can then integrate the question into the topic discussion to facilitate the connections students are making about the content.

Step 4: Find the Root Cause

As discussed earlier, we know that off-task behaviors, whether obvious or subtle, may have one or more of the following root causes. The students

- Do not know what to do or how to do it.
- Do not find the task meaningful, relevant, or interesting.
- Lack a variety of ways to interact with the content.
- Do not feel a sense of belonging in the classroom.
- Lack a sense of autonomy or capacity for self-monitoring.

As Venessa got to know her distracted student, the 12th grader in her science class, she learned that problems at home had left lingering emotions for this student, possibly contributing to her wandering mind. But teachers can do little about a student's home difficulties. A root cause is something a teacher *can* do something about, and so Venessa needed to find a root cause that she could influence. She could now test her hypothesis. If she reduced the density of her words, the student should be on task.

Interviewing students can often help a teacher find the root cause. Consider this example. Venessa is directing the class to read an article on the computer and take notes on it for the next 15 minutes. Students quiet down, and she sits at her desk, hoping to send some quick email responses to parents and administrators.

But she hears chatter in the room; she looks up to see some students whispering and others looking around. One student is not taking notes; their eyes are on the computer screen, but they do not appear to move. Venessa hypothesizes that the student's attention interference is *intrusions*.

Venessa gives up on her email time. She walks over to the student, bends down so each of them can look at the screen at the same eye level, and starts an exploratory conversation to find the root cause:

> Teacher: Show me what sentence you are on.
>
> Student points to the end of the third sentence in the first paragraph.
>
> Teacher: What did you read about before you stopped reading? [Venessa acknowledges the student stopped, reflecting her hypothesis about intrusions.]
>
> Student reads the third sentence again.
>
> Teacher: Why do you think you stopped right there? [Offer options: Were you thinking of something else? Didn't you understand it? Maybe it was boring?]
>
> Student: I don't get it.
>
> Teacher: Well, let's see how I can understand it first.
>
> Teacher reads the title aloud: "Prices and Wages in a Market Economy."
>
> Student watches teacher read the title aloud.
>
> Teacher: That title makes me wonder how wages are set for workers. Maybe there is something in the paragraph about how employers set wages. I recall you work at a hardware store on weekends. Does it make you curious about how your wages were set?
>
> Student: Yeah, I guess [with a shrug].

Teacher: So how about doing something simple before reading? Draw four boxes on your paper.

Student draws four boxes.

Teacher: Now find one interesting thing from the first paragraph, and put it in the first box. Then find one interesting thing from the second paragraph, and put that in the second box. Then do the same with the third and fourth paragraphs. OK?

Student: OK.

Teacher: I'll take a walk around the classroom and then check on your first box.

Student moves their eyes from the boxes to the first paragraph, leans forward, and flips a pencil back and forth while reading.

Venessa walks around the room, stopping to check in with other students who appear off task—sometimes with a nod, or an "All good?" or a "Show me where you are." By the time the teacher returns, the student has written two things in box 1 and one in box 2. Venessa says, "Tell me about that first item in box 2." The student reads it, and Venessa nods approval and leaves. The student turns to the second paragraph to get the second item for box 2.

In this example, Venessa quickly ascertained that the student's mind was wandering; she took the student at their word—that they didn't understand what to do; and then she tested a strategy for this root cause of not understanding. She then returned to see that the student was, in fact, attending to the task. This approach helped assess inattention on the spot.

We've been talking about attention in terms of individual students, but students operate in a group environment. How can we use what we know for individuals to assess attention in classrooms and small groups?

Assessing Off-Task Behavior Patterns Across the Classroom

It seems that every time you turn your back on the class to write instructions on the board (antecedent), your students erupt in talking (obvious off-task behaviors). You feel frustrated; you tell your colleagues that these students don't care about school and just don't pay attention. But then you remember that these are biases, and a solution is to think of attention as an effect, not a cause—and that you have steps at your disposal to assess that inattention.

You hypothesize that the students want peer attention. They're typically in static lessons without interactions with their peers; you propose that the lack of such interactions may be the root cause of their sudden eruptions of talking. To test this hypothesis, you build a peer task with the prompt: "What were two key points from the lesson that you want to recall for the assignment?" You ask the students to think about this, discuss it with their peers, and then share their thoughts in a follow-up discussion on the assignment.

This may work for some and not for others. But this assessment is about *patterns*. Here's another example:

1. The teacher sees students with heads down on their desk or staring out the window and hears them chattering quietly.
2. The teacher notices that this behavior always happens after she gives them instructions to work on an assignment.
3. The teacher hypothesizes that they are avoiding the task.
4. The teacher determines that the reason for the avoidance is that students don't know what to do or how to do it.

Finding Patterns in Groups

The following steps will guide you in finding patterns for small groups or across a classroom.

Step 1. Label the off-task behavior. What are the common behaviors? They could be obvious, such as lots of students talking or getting out of their seats, or subtle, such as lots of students looking around the room or having their heads down on the desk.

Step 2. Observe the behavior. You may notice a lot of talking after recess or after students get into groups for a group project. Students may be late to one period after they have a certain teacher before you, or they may put their heads down on their desk while you write math problems on the board. Consider time of day or any behavior of yours that takes place just before common off-task behaviors. What happens after that behavior of yours? Keep notes to tally your observations:

- On what day does this occur and at what time?
- What's the context of the common off-task behavior? What happens before and after?
- What are the physical dimensions of the behavior: how frequent, how long, and how intense is it?

In the previous section, the teacher focused on one individual student first, the one at the computer, but she also walked around the classroom to continue her assessment before following up with that student. She observed some patterns of off-task behavior, such as students looking around, whispering to a peer, and staring at the paper or computer. She kept a mental tally. She wrote on her notepad that six students were looking around for half the time. Next, she considered the immediate reason for the off-task behaviors. Were those students similar to the initial student who had attention interferences related to not knowing what to do or how to do it?

Step 3. Hypothesize the cause. If you see a lot of movement, it might be because students have been sitting for a long time, so this behavior may be sensory. Or perhaps there's a lot of talking going on after you give directions, so that may point to task avoidance. Or, if students are getting out of their seats to look outside at the same time every day, they could be distracted by something going on there, such as other students playing basketball.

You learned from assessing individual students that off-task behaviors are not due to the same immediate reasons or the same root causes as other students. But you can make hypotheses about the immediate reasons—for example, that students are off task because they're avoiding the work, want attention from you or their peers, or are distracted or having intrusions.

Step 4. Find the root cause. You give an instruction and the class is off task, seemingly avoiding the work. You ask whether they know what to do and how to do it. With a small group or with individual students, you can try a strategy to break apart the assignment into steps. This is something we'll go over shortly in Chapter 3.

Assessing Inattention During Small-Group Activities

Let's now look at how a high school math teacher, Reginald, assesses off-task behavior in his classroom. His previous experience teaching in an elementary school had shown him that setting up his classroom in stations increased student attention because the stations provided a variety of ways to learn. Reginald figured that his older students would need a variety of options, just as his 4th graders did. He set up five stations in his classroom for his 32 students, each with a specific activity: (1) microteaching with Reginald; (2) peer microteaching; (3) silent work on math problems; (4) paired work on a specific issue; and (5) peer prediction discussion on current math work and the upcoming lessons.

Reginald was excited to have matched student needs with the right stations, but although some students thrived in the stations, the groupings did not go as planned. For example, at the peer microteaching station, two students were talking about the topic, but others in the group were looking around the room, doodling, or talking about unrelated topics. In the silent group completing math problems, one student started right away, but others turned toward a friend or looked at the paper and started to doodle or write something unrelated to math.

Reginald decided to interview one group, the peer microteaching group, to assess one set of off-task behaviors. Before starting, Reginald needed to define for himself what he expected to see in terms of on-task behaviors, why he expected to see them, and what off-task behaviors might suggest about *why* the students were off task.

The ideal on-task behavior in the peer microteaching group would look as follows: One student, assigned as the teacher, would demonstrate and conduct a think-aloud of a math problem, with other students watching. The peer teacher would use a large handheld whiteboard to make each step visible. Students could listen to the peer teacher and glance at the whiteboard while working on the problem themselves before the peer completed the think-aloud.

Why is this the ideal on-task behavior? Students can both see and hear the problem before they attempt solving it themselves. The options allow them to choose to attend to the task, ignore distractions, and sustain their attention on it.

What are the common off-task behaviors? They might include looking around the room, chatting with a peer, writing about an unrelated topic, doodling, or leaving the group.

What are potential hypotheses for those off-task behaviors? That the student either wants to escape from the task or get peer attention.

What is a likely root cause? It could be any of the five root causes of off-task behavior: The students don't know what to do or how to do it; the task does not have meaning for them; they lack a variety of ways to interact with the content; they do not feel as though they belong; or they lack a sense of autonomy or capacity for self-regulation.

Reginald carefully placed himself where he could observe, interview students, and make decisions about inattention and strategies. Let's look at this process in more detail.

Observation and interview. Reginald walks over to the peer microteaching group; this is the group where students were engaged in such off-task behaviors as looking around the room, doodling, or talking about unrelated topics. Reginald pulls up a chair to get at eye level with the students and looks at the task on the table in front of them. He asks one student to point to the part of the problem that they understand and to explain what they understand about it. The student says they used the rule of addition as a first step in simplifying the expression. The teacher then asks another student to point to a part of the problem that they understand; the student responds by pointing to the same step and repeating what the first student said, although that student has completed more steps in the problem. Finally, when asked the same question, a third student simply points to the same part of the problem; this student has not completed that part yet.

Hypothesis. Reginald realized that the first two students *were* on task as they did work on the problem themselves. But the students engaged in off-task behaviors because they had already made progress. Reginald hypothesized that these two students didn't have the self-monitoring to move to new or more challenging problems. The third student's off-task behavior might be because the student may not understand the steps because they could not repeat them back, or they might not know how to do what the peer teacher is modeling.

Quick strategy. To test both hypotheses (lack of self-monitoring for two students and doesn't know what to do or how for the third), Reginald offers a quick strategy. He provides additional math problems and assigns each student a specific role: the checker monitors accuracy during the modeling, the questioner clarifies the steps, and the drawer represents the problem in a more creative way on paper.

Agreement. The teacher makes sure all students know their roles, and he asks the students to give a thumbs-up to show they agree to play those roles.

Follow-up. Reginald asks the peer teacher to begin modeling the lesson. He tells the students he will check back shortly to see which step and problem they're on.

When Reginald returns to ask students where they are with the task, one shows their drawing of the problem and the math rules, and another says they have completed three problems. Reginald notices the same off-task student is not drawing, questioning, or looking at the whiteboard, so he asks the student if they want to move to the paired workstation for the next five minutes to work with a student who needs a partner on the same problems from the micro-teaching group. This will enable Reginald to observe and find out what the student doesn't understand and whether the peer can help. Satisfied with some increased attention among the rest of the group, Reginald asks for a thumbs-up that they are still following their roles, then links the new student pair and moves to check on the rest of the groups.

Reginald documents the behaviors of each student he observed and then talks with individual students, letting them know that he wants to understand more about the group's work. In the interview questions, Reginald asks specifically about the lesson the peer teacher taught. This encourages the student to think back to the actual task, rather than to possible interferences. Figure 2.7 describes what he discovered about the six students in the microteaching group.

FIGURE 2.7
Peer Microteaching: Five Student Behaviors

Behavior	Assumption	Interview Data and Potential Root Causes
Talking to a peer—related topic	External on-topic interference (interruption)	**Student A** was talking to a peer about the math problem. **Why?** Because the student completed the problem and was telling a friend how to do the problem.
Talking to a peer—unrelated topic	External off-topic interference (distraction)	**Student B** was gossiping to someone about their friends. **Why?** Because the student had already completed the problem.
Looking around the room	External off-topic interference (distraction)	**Student C** was listening to other students talk and was looking at them. **Why?** Because the student was too far away from the whiteboard to see the problem.
Drawing	Internal off-topic interference (intrusion)	**Student D** was sketching a picture of a dog. **Why?** Because although the student was listening to the peer, they were unsure of the steps in the problem.
Writing	Internal on-topic interference (diversion)	**Student E** was writing down the problem while listening to the peer. **Why?** Because writing helped the student listen to the demonstration.

After interviewing and making assumptions about root causes, Reginald found four different patterns in the data. These revealed that some students (1) could not see the problem on the whiteboard; (2) did not understand the problem or the steps in the problem; (3) learned by writing while listening; or (4) had already completed the problem. He concluded that some students did not need to see the whiteboard and learned better by writing while listening. Others needed to understand more before the demonstration to move to a more challenging problem, or they needed to find a different way to see the problem during the demonstration. And some students had already completed the work, so they were no longer paying attention.

In this example, Reginald placed himself with his students, observed, interviewed, tested, and monitored. Not all students will pay attention all the time; the goal is simply to create better conditions for attention. Reginald not only met the goal, but also recognized that assessing attention is part of the learning process, one that continually improves conditions for attention.

Conclusion

This chapter presented a systematic way to understand inattention as off-task behavior. The steps are detailed, but they establish a process so that over time you'll be able to do the steps in simpler and quicker ways. When you first notice inattention, or off-task behavior, you will automatically label the behavior and ask why. Then you can observe for potential immediate reasons and likely root causes. Based on this assessment, you will begin to test the strategies offered in Chapter 3.

Chapter Reflection: Rate Your Understanding

This chapter presented a walkthrough of the assessment of attention. The goal is to think systematically and act systematically. In other words, over time you can train yourself to *look* and *listen*. Assessing for attention doesn't punish ("Stop talking!"). It does not judge ("You just don't care about your education!"). Once we look—and ask—we can find likely root causes and start experimenting with strategies for individual students and the entire classroom.

The following reflection questions address each of the main areas of the chapter. Rate your ability as 1, 2, 3, 4, or 5, with 5 being highest.

- How would you rate your skills in addressing the five principles for assessing behavior (assess individuals first, be flexible when defining on-task behavior, differentiate types of off-task behaviors, seek the why, know the assessment goal): 1, 2, 3, 4, or 5? Why did you select that rating?
- How would you rate your skills in performing a four-step procedure for assessing behavior (label the off-task behavior, observe the behavior, hypothesize the cause, find the root cause): 1, 2, 3, 4, or 5? Why did you select that rating?

- How would you rate your skills in finding one of the four immediate reasons from behavioral psychology (escape from task, sensory stimulation, attention seeking, tangible reward) for obvious off-task behaviors: 1, 2, 3, 4, or 5? Why did you select that rating?
- How would you rate your skills in identifying one of the four immediate reasons based on cognitive psychology (diversions, interruptions, intrusions, distractions) for subtle off-task behaviors: 1, 2, 3, 4, or 5? Why did you select that rating?
- How would you rate your skills in determining a likely root cause of off-task behavior: 1, 2, 3, 4, or 5? Why did you select that rating?
- How would you rate your skills in assessing off-task behavior patterns across the classroom: 1, 2, 3, 4, or 5? Why did you select that rating?

Consider starting your assessments in areas where you rated yourself as strong. For areas you rated yourself lower on, develop questions that target what you need to know more about, then go back to that section in the chapter to find your answers.

Learn More: Functional Behavior Assessment

Behavior research has found four immediate reasons for obvious off-task behaviors; we have referred to them as *escape from task*, *sensory stimulation*, *attention seeking*, and *tangible reward*. These findings have been replicated over time for all kinds of behaviors, from self-injurious behaviors to general off-task student behaviors in the classroom. The process of deciding on one of these four reasons, or functions, is often called a functional behavior assessment (FBA).

In an FBA, a school team will gather data from multiple sources, from teachers as well as caretakers, and use multiple methods, such as more structured observations, interviews, or rating scales. Here are some interview questions you can use to probe a student about a behavior; they're adapted from Witt and colleagues (2000). This example uses the behavior of getting out of one's seat.

- I'd like to talk with you about getting out of your seat. Do you see this as a problem?
- When did this first start?
- Did anything happen that got this behavior started?
- Why do you get out of your seat?

- What usually happens when you get out of your seat? (antecedents and consequences)
- What might you do instead?
- What would help you do that?

More formal assessments are also available. The Motivation Assessment Scale (MAS) (Durand & Crimmins, 1988, 1992; Haim, 2002) is a 51-item questionnaire with Likert-scale responses that can determine how often an individual's target behavior occurs in a particular context. Responses are calculated in subscales aligned to escape from task or from attention, sensory stimulation, attention seeking, and tangible reward and show the most likely reason for the target behavior. The Functional Assessment Checklist for Teachers and Staff (FACTS) (March et al., 2000) is a two-page interview that gathers information about the target behavior, routines, context, and antecedents and consequences.

A situation needing more data may require the involvement of multiple school personnel. For example, you may be asked to participate in an FBA as part of a student's special education evaluation. If a student is displaying the problem behavior across school contexts, the school team may use the FBA as the basis for creating a behavior intervention plan. Likewise, if there are problematic and persistent individual behaviors in your classroom, you probably want to involve a school team that includes a school psychologist or behavior specialist. These colleagues can help with multiple methods in multiple settings—in different classrooms, in academic or physical education settings, at school, and at home.

3

Five Principles
for Promoting Attention

When teacher Adrienne Hayes was in 3rd grade, her class was watching a science video. It was in the afternoon, she recalled, and her mind had been wandering. The teacher stopped the video and asked Adrienne a question. She couldn't answer and felt embarrassed in front of her peers.

When she first started teaching, Adrienne did the same thing to one of her students. Right after she asked the student the question, she realized they had been slouching in their seat, possibly absorbed in something else—and perhaps that's why she had singled them out. Just then, Adrienne recalled, "I realized that my 3rd grade teacher had noticed from *my* body language that I wasn't paying attention, so she targeted me as a 'gotcha.'" Adrienne never did that again.

High school teacher Sean Miller made a similar observation. When a student didn't seem to be paying attention, he would call on them, saying, "Hey, what do you think?" Years later, he reflects, "I got away from doing that. It was like a 'gotcha' in a public setting."

Adrienne and Sean knew from personal experience that calling out inattentive students is a punishment rather than a learning opportunity. Unsurprisingly, the "gotcha" causes stress in students and can produce the opposite effect on attention (Crozier, 1998; Hoy & Weinstein, 2013). Recognizing that this approach was ineffective, Adrienne and Sean learned to stop and assess attention first. What are the off-task behaviors? Why might they be occurring?

Chapter 2 revealed five common root causes of inattention. Here, we pair those root causes with *five principles for promoting attention*. Students are inattentive because they

- Do not know what to do or how to do it. *Principle for promoting attention*: reduce cognitive load.
- Do not find the task meaningful, relevant, or interesting. *Principle for promoting attention*: incorporate students' background knowledge.
- Lack a variety of ways to interact with the content. *Principle for promoting attention*: integrate multiple modalities.
- Do not feel a sense of belonging in the classroom. *Principle for promoting attention*: nurture positive relationships.
- Lack a sense of autonomy or capacity for self-monitoring. *Principle for promoting attention*: teach self-regulation.

By definition, a root cause is likely the best reason for the off-task behavior, and it is a problem we can fix. And how do we fix it? By *creating conditions for attention*. This means recognizing root causes and knowing the practices effective in addressing them. Such knowledge enables teachers to develop a range of strategies to "fix" off-task behavior.

To create conditions for attention, we'll draw on those five general principles for addressing root causes of inattention (see Figure 3.1). These principles incorporate strategies you can use, adapt, and supplement in the classroom.

- **Reduce cognitive load.** Students may find the information too plentiful or too difficult for them. They may escape the task by letting their mind wander or by physically moving away from the task. Strategies for reducing cognitive load—the amount of information in working memory—will help students attend to the concepts and work through the tasks.
- **Incorporate students' background knowledge.** Students may not find the content meaningful. If they are uninterested, they may shift their attention to more interesting off-task behaviors. Incorporating student background knowledge into content will encourage students to attend to what they find relevant about the task.
- **Integrate multiple modalities.** Students may be engaging in tasks through linguistic interaction alone. They may be seeking sensory variety by doodling, moving around the classroom, or talking with their peers. Introducing multiple modes of engagement can encourage students to pay attention and learn in a variety of ways.

- **Nurture positive relationships.** Students may not feel that they belong or have any agency in the classroom. They may feel unseen and unheard. Their minds may wander, or they may seek attention from peers or adults in negative ways. Building positive relationships throughout the year will encourage attention by fostering a sense of belonging.
- **Teach self-regulation.** Students may not have learned to monitor their own behavior. They may easily be distracted by attention interferences, tuning in to their own feelings or other distractors. Teaching students skills for self-regulation can help them voluntarily monitor—and self-correct—their own attention.

Let's take a deeper look at these principles and some strategies based on them that you can incorporate in your classroom.

FIGURE 3.1
Five Principles for Promoting Attention

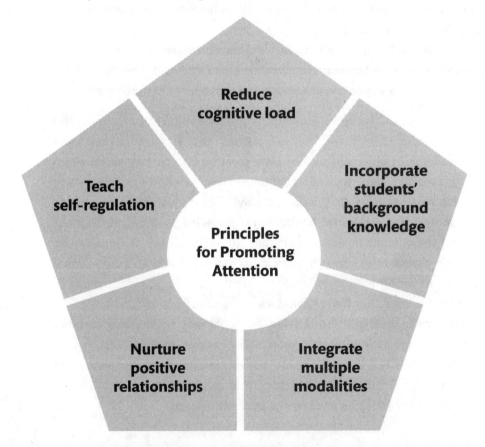

Attention Principle 1: Reduce Cognitive Load

In 1989, British American rapper Young MC released "Busta Move." At the end of the first refrain, he calls out, "Break it down for me, fellas!" What follows is a new beat and a sequence of short sounds. The listener's attention must suddenly reorient to them. You've probably noticed the change in whole-class attention when you paused after a long explanation to write three quick ideas or steps on the board. Maybe it's not as interesting as the shift in a song that won a Grammy Award, but it's effective for attention nonetheless.

As the song requests, let me break it down for you. *Cognitive load* is our total mental capacity to think through a topic we're focused on. This mental effort occurs within working memory, the cognitive process activated after initial attention (Baddeley, 1992; Engle, 2018).

Extraneous cognitive load is **too much information** for students' working memory. The students may be listening to and watching a teacher who is talking for a long period of time; somewhere they got lost or missed an idea, and now their minds are wandering. Without any steps, visual cues, or references to the purpose of the work, the information feels superfluous or nonessential. The information needs to be broken down.

Intrinsic cognitive load means the information or task is **too difficult** for students. They may lack the necessary skills, but it could also be that they simply find the task overwhelming. They need the content and steps to be broken down.

Too much information—or information that is too difficult—can produce a high cognitive load that interferes with choosing to attend or sustaining attention (Lavie, 1995; Lavie et al., 2004). The following strategies address extraneous and intrinsic cognitive load by breaking it down.

Talk Less

Do you talk too much? Teachers do, taking up to an average of 89 percent of classroom time (Hattie, 2012). They might explain a task and then decide to explain it in different ways, or they may describe many points about a topic without pausing. But as talking continues, on-task behavior declines; research shows that the lowest rates of on-task behavior occur when teachers are standing in front of the class. The fact is, when teachers talk less, students engage more (Godwin et al., 2013, 2016; Hattie, 2012).

During whole-group instruction, there are many ways you can remind yourself to use fewer words. One strategy is **wait time**, pausing after asking a question and allowing students to think about it before answering. For example, after writing three concepts on the board, the teacher might ask students what they know about the first one and then wait for students to respond before moving on to the second concept. This enables students to reorient from attention interferences back to the topic and to think before they or their peers respond. You can introduce more pauses to encourage attention before repeating, summarizing, or asking a different question.

Let's say that the teacher has now been talking for about five minutes on a topic. While talking, the teacher notices that some students have put their heads on their desks; some are slouched in their seats, looking at the ground; and some are playing with pens or other objects. The teacher switches abruptly from a discussion of the topic to a task direction:

> Teacher: Now take out your books and turn to page 56 to read what we just talked about. Make sure you use the visual organizer I just distributed.
>
> Student: What are we supposed to do again?
>
> Other students look at one another, one starts whispering, another gets up, some start shuffling to get their books.
>
> Teacher: What I said was, get out your book…
>
> As the teacher starts talking more slowly and raising their voice, more students start talking, and the teacher speaks even louder over the growing noise in the room.

This teacher meant well by explaining all about the topic and then telling the students what they needed to do next to learn. But students' subtle off-task behaviors showed inattention as the teacher talked. Their body positions changed at the teacher's task command, with many alternating their attention between the off-task behavior and the teacher and others noticing a break when they could talk to their friends. The teacher was understandably frustrated at the students' behavior, especially after having put energy into explaining the topic.

What could the teacher have done instead? Even speaking for a shorter amount of time—three minutes instead of five—can help. During these three minutes, the teacher can follow a **rule of three** (Carlson & Shu, 2007) as a way to cluster complex ideas. They can

- **Organize** phrases into three main points;
- **Say** that there are three main points;
- **Gesture** that there are three main points;
- **Write** the three points on the board; or
- **Draw** three shapes around the main points as a transition to the assignment.

When it's time to direct students to a task, use a **transition phrase** like this: "I'm going to summarize these three points. Then I'll tell you the steps to take to dig deeper into these three points, one at a time."

To get used to talking less, you might want to experiment with using shorter phrases, connecting the phrases with gestures and visuals, and checking in with your students about their attention: "Where did I lose you?" By talking less, we assume responsibility for improving communication to help get students back on task.

Chunk Content and Time

Chunking means taking a lot of information and breaking it into parts. Think about the following:

- What information can I divide into smaller pieces to present?
- How can I cut this reading or general content into shorter pieces?
- How can I encourage students to attend to just one piece at a time?
- What are good chunks of time to use for a student to make some small amount of progress?

In the past, art teacher Kevin Wilson taught three aesthetic theories at the same time about how we judge art: imitationalism, formalism, and emotionalism. He noticed over time that this was too much information to give students all at once and that student attention waned. So he started chunking the three approaches.

First, Kevin told students to look at specific images in a book, as if they were looking at art pieces in a museum. After they discussed the images, he asked a guiding question: "What art should I use imitationalism to judge?" Students guessed various art pieces. Kevin then wrote the criteria for imitationalism on the board and rephrased the question: "For which art piece would I use imitationalism the most?" Students started using the criteria as evidence for their choices.

One at a time, Kevin added the other two aesthetic theories, ending with the most complex approach: using more than one theory at a time to judge art. Kevin chunked the information in small enough pieces that it was manageable for students, and he saw selective and sustained attention increase.

In elementary schools, teachers use many chunking strategies as students develop reading skills. One example is **phrase slashes**, where the teacher or students draw a forward slash between phrases within sentences and double slashes between sentences. Students then practice fluent reading one phrase at a time. Students might also number sentences within paragraphs or draw a box around a paragraph, making a note about the takeaway in the margin.

If you're just getting started with chunking content in this way, a list of basic **annotations** can help. These might include a check mark to indicate something the student already knows, a star for something interesting to follow up on, a question mark for something the student doesn't understand, and a heart for a phrase the student really likes. Practice with one or two at a time, and see what other marks students devise on their own and for what purpose.

It's not just early readers who benefit from chunks in reading. Adults also rely on working memory to hold a string of words together to understand a sentence. For example, if a sentence is too long, with too many technical words or words that are new to me, my mind may wander, and I may need to return to the beginning of the sentence, using my own annotation marks to clarify main points.

Time can also be chunked. Fourth grade teacher Adrienne Hayes notices different kinds of mind-wandering in her class. When it's close to a break, lunch, or the end of the day, Adrienne asks students what they are thinking about. Some will say, "For lunch, I have…" whereas some of her "deep thinkers" in math might respond, "I'm just trying to figure out this problem." She sees they need more time to think about the task. When asking questions that require a bit of reflection, she has students use a timer, saying, for example, "See what you can do in two minutes" or "Think about the concept, and check in with me in five minutes. Be sure you set your timer."

Chunking both content and time helps manage cognitive load. To chunk content, a teacher might say, "Add at least two similarities and two differences in your Venn diagram," waiting until most students have added at least two before moving on to the next step. Depending on the task, the teacher might suggest time limits, such as, "Talk with your partner for two minutes" about a topic or "Start the task and mark where you are in seven minutes." A **visual timer,** also called a 60-minute timer, is commonly used in schools; it's large enough for students to see and shows the amount of time left in a red area that diminishes as the timer counts down. Some teachers use mobile devices or a kitchen timer, and others let students use their own mobile phone or device.

Create Stepping Stones

You're a student, standing with your teacher in front of a platform that is about eye level to you. You can't see any steps going up to the platform. The teacher says, "Get up on that platform. Then we'll get started." What do you do?

A. You turn around, walk away, and say, "This is stupid."
B. You ignore the request and start daydreaming about somewhere you would rather be.
C. You look at the teacher, waiting for more guidance.
D. You turn away from the teacher and start talking to other students.

This is a metaphor for a task that a teacher tells a student to start doing. As in many task directions, there are no steps: "Do this reading," "Solve this problem," "Find the answer." The student does not know how to do the task and responds with off-task behaviors that are both obvious (leaving, talking) and subtle (looking away). A better approach would be for the teacher to build steps in the first place so that students can go up the stairs themselves to reach the platform.

Stepping stones are particularly helpful for addressing *intrinsic cognitive load*—the task's inherent difficulty—because they break the complex task down into simple pieces, enabling students to pay attention to each step. Stepping stones may call to mind the term *scaffolding* (Bruner, 1966); there, the teacher supports students at each level of learning so that they can ultimately climb to the most challenging one.

The approach is helpful in reading. Students can take a series of steps toward independent reading, from practicing with the whole class (**choral reading**) or in pairs (**paired reading**), to reading aloud to themselves while listening to an audio recording, to reading aloud to others. These reading fluency stepping stones move from simple (phrase slashes) to complex (reading aloud to others).

Simple-to-complex stepping stones can also support students in math. Ayres (2006) studied whether students benefited from simple-to-complex sequencing in a typical algebra task with a high cognitive load: the order of operations. One group of students learned each part of the order of operations, which the teacher introduced step by step. A second group learned the entire math problem and the related steps all at the same time, and a third group used a mixed approach. Students with lower math problem-solving skills were more on task with the stepping stones, and students overall performed better with the stepping stones and the mixed approach.

These simple-to-complex approaches have been studied in other domains. Researchers have looked at the effectiveness of teaching spreadsheet skills before having students do mathematical calculations within spreadsheets (Clarke et al., 2005) and of teaching the individual components of a mechanical system before tackling how the components function together (Mayer et al., 2002). Our art teacher, Kevin Wilson, also chunked from simple to complex in his approach to teaching aesthetic theories. As students practiced each theory separately, he layered in questions about the other theories, such as, "What is one thing a formalist would say about that image, and what is one thing an emotionalist would say?"

Applying these strategies in the classroom also proceeds from simple to complex. Practice using short phrases in the aim of talking less, or start with having students use just a few annotations. Just as with stepping stones for students, start small and then move on.

Lessen External Interferences

Have you ever tried using a **focus mode** on your computer while working to remove distractions coming from other computer applications? The idea is to remove excess audio and visual input so that irrelevant information doesn't interfere with what you're manipulating in your working memory while typing, thus avoiding an increase in extrinsic cognitive load.

As discussed in Chapter 2, external interferences are called *distractions,* if they are off topic, or *interruptions*, if they are on topic. The goal in reducing external interferences is to remove the extraneous, even if it is on topic, such as a relevant **wall display** showing whale habitats while students listen to a story about whales. You want their focus to remain on the story.

Researchers tested the effect of wall displays on the attention and task performance of kindergartners. They set up two classrooms with different wall displays: one classroom was decorated with pictures, maps, student artwork, and images of the solar system and dolphins; the other classroom had a few objects on mostly empty shelves and nothing on the walls. The students sat in a semicircle during two weeks in each of the two classrooms, engaging in six five- to seven-minute read-alouds on science topics they were unfamiliar with (bugs, flight, plate tectonics, the solar system, and volcanoes).

Results showed that in both conditions, students were on task 66 percent of the time. But there was a significant difference in the *pattern* of focus in each condition. Students spent more time off task and were more frequently distracted in the highly decorated classroom. Post-tests on the science content showed that students in the decorated classroom had significantly lower scores than those in the less decorated room (Fisher et al., 2014).

This does not mean that classroom walls should be bare. Instead, it means that teachers should avoid displaying irrelevant visuals. Using measures of eye tracking, researchers have shown that as eyes start looking at irrelevant visuals, attention to the topic at hand wanes (Choi et al., 2014). To test whether visuals are necessary, just ask yourself whether the images—stripped of their words—convey the message you want to convey. If they don't, remove them.

A simple way to consider external interferences is to choose carefully what goes on the walls of your classroom. Consider which items are likely to be more distracting than helpful to students. Which common routines would your students benefit from seeing daily on the classroom walls? Which student work will you display and for how long? What other displays would be useful references for your students?

Incorporate students' background knowledge

Attention Principle 2: Incorporate Students' Background Knowledge

Using an eye-tracking monitor, researcher Tanya Kaefer studied the visual attention of 41 kindergarten students while they looked at storybooks on familiar and unfamiliar topics. Students who had more background knowledge about the topic more quickly alternated their attention to the visuals and accompanying words (Kaefer, 2018). Kaefer's further research showed that, although building prior knowledge before the task helped with attention, it was even more important to include students' own background knowledge (Kaefer, 2020).

Consider your own experiences. What books do you pick up? What do you investigate online? Why do you choose those books or websites? What background knowledge or experiences do you have that relate to that topic?

Whatever your answer, you will always find some connection to existing schema. In cognitive psychology, *schema* is an organized mental structure for a topic. To learn, we activate our existing schema (what we already know) about a topic, then we ask questions, gathering new information to build on what we know. Schema theory posits that learning occurs as conflicts between the new and the known resolve, resulting in the reconstruction of our schema—in other words, new knowledge (Piaget, 1952, 1954).

From schema theory to education studies in domains like literacy and culturally responsive teaching, we know that students are more on task when the topics connect to them. Their background is not only what they already know, but also what they have understood and experienced, which enables them to see themselves in the content (Kintsch, 1998). This can include learning fractions or decimals through cooking or shopping, tying a current event to a historical one, or choosing children's books with main characters that look like your students (Gay, 2018; Howard & Terry, 2011; Ladson-Billings, 1997).

Integrating this background knowledge helps promote selective attention (Kim & Rehder, 2011), provides cues to reorient students' attention to the task (Lambert, 2003), and offers meaning and relevance to sustain attention (Shell & Flowerday, 2019). We need to know our students for this integration to occur—their thoughts and interests, their lives outside school, their cultures. Here are some ways to do so.

Interview Students

What are the cultural backgrounds of your students? Where have they lived? With whom do they live and interact? What are their life experiences? An informal but planned **interview** is one strategy for finding out more about your students. Before interviewing, invite the student to talk with you. For example, "Would you mind if we sit down for 20 minutes, and I interview you about what you like? I'm interviewing students to get to know them," or "Could I have your permission to ask you a few questions about your interests?" Invitations that enable the student to agree (or disagree) support student agency in having a positive discussion, and students are often intrigued by having an adult pay attention just to them.

The interview questions that follow focus on a range of experiences and on whether students do these activities alone or with others (adapted from

Wisniewski et al., 2012). You can adapt the questions according to what you want to know, what the student starts to talk about, and what other topics the conversation opens.

- What do you read? What books? What types of magazines or news? What comics? What websites do you like?
- What do you do on the computer or your phone or tablet? What social media do you use (e.g., Snapchat, TikTok, Instagram, Twitter/X)? What video games do you play?
- What TV or media do you watch (e.g., TV, YouTube, Hulu, Netflix)? What show did you watch recently?
- What music do you listen to? What songs? What artists?
- What sports or sports teams do you like?
- What other activities do you like? What outdoor games? What trading cards? What board games? Do you like to draw, sing, do art, or play an instrument?
- Who do you spend the most time with? What activities do you do together? Who do you like to [name an activity] with?
- What interested you most in what we've talked about?
- What would you like me to ask you that I haven't asked you yet?
- Do you have any questions for me?

These questions are low risk; they ask about activities and behaviors, rather than student perspectives on them. But from listening to students' responses, you can gauge what they like most or what they feel uncomfortable with so you can decide how to follow up. For example, if a student tells you about a role-playing video game in great detail, but their other answers are brief, follow-up questions might get at how the game characters are connected, how they relate to the student's own perspectives, or how the student might turn a particular academic task into a game. The last three questions listed could reveal the student's priority interest, and they show that you're open to additional sharing, as well as to their questions.

Other interview questions can come from investigating what Luis Moll calls "funds of knowledge," or student assets from outside school. Sample categories of assets are economics, geography, politics, agriculture, technology, religion, language, and cooking (González et al., 2005; Moll et al., 1992). These can be explored through questions like, What is your home language? What are some of your family values or traditions? What are some of your household chores? What educational activities does your family enjoy? What jobs do your family members do? After getting to know students, take the next step to integrate what you learn into lessons, basing them on student cultures, interests, and background knowledge and experiences.

Plan Lessons with Student Experiences in Mind

Getting to know students one by one enables teachers to build personal and cultural references across the whole class. When the COVID-19 pandemic affected the first full year of schooling, Nycole Bradshaw used cooking to teach fractions to 6th graders. She knew that learning fractions was challenging for students. She recalled, "Fractions are the bane of their existence. The average student doesn't like anything less than a whole number—or greater than a whole number and not directly the next whole number." She noted that many students preferred to look around the room or do anything other than participate in a fractions lesson.

She decided to draw on cooking, something students did every day at home, as well as bring in some realities from the pandemic. She had students set a goal: to make a recipe for 15 essential workers. They discussed who essential workers were—hospital staff, firefighters, and so on—and then students chose a recipe with at least five ingredients, with two in fractional form. The goal was to convert a recipe that served 2–4 people into one that served 15. The project took place over the two weeks before Thanksgiving break and continued into the following week, enabling students to cook with family over the break and then return to the project.

Nycole said the project was so successful in capturing student attention that she continued teaching fractions with recipes as more students returned to in-person learning. Integrating what students do at home makes the content meaningful. In math, for example, the class can measure distances between local places or compare the amount of sugar and vitamins in two different cereals.

Encouraging students to **share experiences** is another strategy. In Marissa Coppock's 8th grade social studies class, some students frequently talked to one another; some had their heads down on the desk or looked around constantly; and yet others appeared restless, getting up or moving around their seats. She took her problem to Ash Hall, the special education teacher and behavior specialist, to find out what to do about the pervasive classroom inattention.

The two of them decided to get to know students by first looking at the class demographics. Of the 27 students in the class, 11 were newcomers from

Mexico. Three of those were recently in child detention centers at the border. Marissa quickly realized that she had been teaching U.S. history from the perspective of European explorers, ignoring the perspectives of Indigenous people from Mexico whose culture and lives had been appropriated when the United States seized one-third of Mexican land in the Mexican-American War.

After doing this simple demographic review, Marissa asked students to share their experiences in class. Students talked about their extended winter breaks with their families in Mexico and El Salvador, travels to and from the United States, and events important to their families. By using the information to create lessons and prompts for writing exercises, Marissa did away with the pervasive inattention.

Connect the New with the Known

Think of everything as needing a connection. The **last/first** writing strategy is a good example: when you write a paragraph, generally your next sentence builds on the last thought of the previous one. Similarly, students need to connect new information to known information. If there is no obvious good connection to the previous knowledge, **K-W-L** is a good way to generate information students already know (Ogle, 1986). Students ask themselves what they Know (K), what they Want to know (W), and, after a learning experience, what they Learned (L).

Donna M. Ogle published the K-W-L strategy in 1986, one of the first in education based on schema theory. Typically, teachers show a K-W-L chart with three columns and fill it in while modeling what is known, asking students what they already know about the topic: "What do you know about Shakespeare? The Civil War? Water? The sky?" Fourth grade teacher Adrienne Hayes uses K-W-L in a six-week lesson on animals; she first models K-W-L by choosing her own animal, a springbok gazelle. She models by thinking aloud about what she already knows about the animal—its habitat, diet, behavior, and reproduction. When it's time for students to choose their own animals for the project, she refers to the K-W-L chart so that students can generate what they already know about a wolf, fish, or bear, for example. Students can ask questions about what they know and call to mind experiences related to the topic before, during, and after engaging with the topic.

Another way to connect with previous information is by using an **advance organizer**. You may know these organizers by other names, such as graphic or visual organizers. An advance organizer is a visual framework used *in advance of*—before—a lesson to help students know what they'll be learning by

organizing concepts to build on throughout the lesson (Ausubel, 1968). The first
30 years of research on advance organizers revealed four types (Marzano, 1998):

- An *expository advance organizer* provides the main categories or ideas
  in the lesson. In the example above, K-W-L helped students identify the
  four categories of animal features they would find in the project. This
  helped organize what is known—or what students think they know—
  before the lesson.
- A *narrative advance organizer* uses a story structure to convey information. A teacher might use it to tell their family's immigration story or to
  tell the story of cell mitosis by personifying parts of the cell and calling
  the cell a house.
- A *graphic advance organizer* visually categorizes information, such as a
  three-ring Venn diagram of similarities and differences among the three
  branches of government or a table of the animal classifications from
  domain through species, with examples of the animals in the unit.
- A *skimming advance organizer* encourages students to review the material using a specific strategy. For example, the class might annotate a
  reading by placing boxes around headings and circles around subhead-
  ings; they can then move the boxed and circled headings to paper to use
  as a visual organizer for adding details while reading or to create questions about the headings before reading.

High school art teacher Kevin Wilson used images to create a narrative
advance organizer in his introduction to art criticism. Kevin presented five
artworks and asked students to order them from least to most appealing.
Students then wrote a rationale for their order, focusing on the least and the
most appealing pieces first. He tallied the results on the board, and students
shared their rationales. Without yet knowing how to critique art, students were
building background knowledge by writing and speaking about what they saw—
something they do every day on social media and in the community.

Expository advance organizers are most common because they offer an
organized way to build and generate background knowledge; for example, the
teacher can create a **vocabulary rating chart** (Beck & Beck-Gernsheim,
2002; Blachowicz, 1986). (See Figure 3.2, which features terminology used in
this book.) The teacher presents vocabulary that will appear in the lesson and
asks students to "rate" their knowledge of the word on a scale from 1 (I don't
know the word or concept) to 4 (I can define and provide an example of the
word or concept).

FIGURE 3.2

Vocabulary Rating Chart for Vocabulary Used in This Book

Vocabulary Rate your familiarity with the term on a scale from 1 to 4.	1 I don't know the word or concept.	2 I have seen or heard of the word or concept.	3 I can define the word or concept.	4 I can define and provide an example of the word or concept.
Selective attention				
Alternating attention				
Sustained attention				
Working memory				
Functional behavior assessment				
Root cause analysis				
Cognitive load				
Background knowledge				
Modalities				
Positive relationships				
Self-regulation				

Whether using K-W-L or advance organizers, an easy way to start connecting the new with the known is to make the guiding question "What do you know about _____?" part of your teaching routine. Students become aware of what they know and of how to build on that knowledge, and they even start to consider the question themselves ("What do *I* know?") as they refine their attention to their own learning.

Build Curiosity

What is cerebral palsy? How do you get cerebral palsy? Is it always the oldest kid in the family who gets cerebral palsy? Are there different types of cerebral palsy? In a classroom example (Brotherson & Santana, 2017), 4th graders have brainstormed 18 questions in preparation to read the book *Out of My Mind* by Sharon Draper (2012), about a young girl with cerebral palsy. The students have selected six of those questions to guide their reading.

Their teacher, Deidre Brotherson, uses the Right Question Institute's **Question Formulation Technique**. First, students produce their own questions using the following rules: (1) ask as many questions as you can; (2) do not stop to judge or answer questions; (3) write down every question as stated; and (4) change any statement into a question. Second, students improve their questions by categorizing the question types as open- or closed-ended, naming the advantages and disadvantages of each, or changing questions from one type to the other. Third, students prioritize questions—here, they selected six to focus on—providing their rationale for choosing them. Finally, students plan how to use their questions in their reading or work (Rothstein & Santana, 2011). Deidre noticed that students were immediately on task when they started their projects, which covered subjects like twins, wheelchair improvements, and a lesson on how to treat people.

The act of asking a question engages attention. Think of a question to ask someone in your family. You're likely to stop reading this book, look away, and think about who you will ask and what the question may be. Your attention is on the question, and the topic is personal to you. In K-W-L, questions purposefully come after generating background knowledge because a reconstructed schema depends on asking questions. Many times, creating meaningful questions (the "W" in K-W-L) is the most challenging part.

When the students of 4th grade teacher Adrienne Hayes get stuck on the W in their animal K-W-L, she turns their attention to the springbok gazelle K-W-L she modeled and asks, "Why did I ask this specific question?" They might answer, "Because you wanted to know more about habitat or the temperament of the animal." "Considering that," she might continue, "what can *you* ask?" Or, noticing that all their questions focus on diet, she might say, "I want you to return to your group and come up with questions in a new category." A follow-up comment helps focus their attention on the task: "Let me know when you have a new question in a new category."

Even informally, questions drive attention. In this example about averages in 5th grade math, the teacher builds on an overheard student conversation about a recent game of the U.S. women's soccer team.

> Teacher: Let's find averages using soccer. Do you want to measure the average amount that a soccer player runs in the game or the average distance of the winning goals?

Students are watching the teacher; some say "kicks," and others talk to one another about running or kicking in soccer. The students are mostly on topic.

Teacher: How about taking a vote?

The teacher then throws out the two options, and most students raise their hands for measuring the average distance of the goal kicks.

Teacher: What question do we need to answer? Turn and talk to your shoulder partner, and write down the question. You have one minute.

Students talk and generate a question. They have done this before, so they know to write the questions in their notebooks and look up when done; some finish but then start talking to their peers.

Teacher: Someone volunteer to ask the question.

The students have done this before, too, and volunteers turn their desk markers to green. The teacher chooses two students to offer their questions.

One student says, "What is the distance of the kicks?" and the other, "How far do they kick in a game?"

The teacher writes both on the board, modeling a think-aloud, and combines the questions to read, "What is the average distance of the goals kicked in the game on Tuesday?"

The teacher connected to student background knowledge and then guided students to create the questions themselves.

Questioning strategies are not new. Manzo (1969, 1970) developed **reciprocal questioning,** in which the teacher models questions and then students ask one another questions at particular points in a reading. First, students read a selection and write questions next to the selection. A good place to start may be just one paragraph. Next, the teacher listens to student questions, but does not answer them. Instead, the teacher acknowledges the questions and might label them, as in, 'This is a question about what will happen next"; "This one is answered in the paragraph"; and "This one connects the reading to a topic outside the text."

The teacher then asks questions that help students answer their own questions and repeats the process for a new section of the reading. When the class is ready to read the rest of the passage, they select purpose-setting questions, such as, Why is the teacher having us read this? Why am I so interested in this? What would make this more interesting? What can I do to make this more understandable? Why are these ideas important to know? Why did the author write this?

Questions create a culture of curiosity, one that relates to what students know and what they want to know more about, making the content meaningful and capturing their attention. However, shifting a classroom culture to make student questioning the norm is not an easy task, especially when students have been taught that answers are more important than questions. Some ways to start are using essential questions derived from standards, turning headings or topic sentences into questions, and asking students to turn a comment into a question.

 Try This: Cognitive Load and Background Knowledge

You can experiment with your own cognitive load and background knowledge needs by doing the following:

1. Go to an open-access article about attention:

- "Attention as an Effect Not a Cause" (Krauzlis et al., 2014), www.ncbi.nlm.nih.gov/pmc/articles/PMC4186707/
- "Attention Matters: How Orchestrating Attention May Relate to Classroom Learning" (Keller et al., 2020), www.ncbi.nlm.nih.gov/pmc/articles/PMC8711818/

2. Start to read the article. The first time you stop in your reading, mark where you stopped; this indicates your first interference, whether it is internal or external.

3. If it is external, start again. If it's internal, take a moment to hypothesize what about the article stopped you. Was there too much information (*extraneous* cognitive load)? Was the information too challenging (*intrinsic* cognitive load)? Did you lack sufficient background information (*germane* cognitive load)? It may be a mix, and that's fine.

4. If you would like to continue, try using strategies like phrase slashes to break apart the sentences and delineate between sentences, or have more fun with it and try paired or choral reading with someone at home or school. Reflect on what you notice about your selective attention (what you choose to attend to,

keeping out interferences) or sustained attention (the duration of your focus on the reading). Afterward, try this self-awareness experiment with your students when they stop reading, and provide options within Principle 1 (reduce cognitive load) or Principle 2 (incorporate students' background knowledge) to help them continue reading.

Integrate
multiple
modalities

Attention Principle 3: Integrate Multiple Modalities

You're sitting in a professional development workshop. The presenter says, "I'm going to say two sentences now, and you can ask me as many questions as you can to figure out the situation they describe." Then the presenter says, "A car pulls up to a hotel. Someone goes bankrupt." Questions start in the room: "Was it a bank robbery?" "Was the car stolen?" "Who was driving the car?" Some people look at their laptops, some watch others ask questions, some look around the room, and some chat quietly with the person next to them.

So, what *is* the situation? Someone is playing the game "Monopoly." This strategy, in which individuals problem solve to come up with creative solutions, is called a **lateral thinking puzzle.**

You've noticed that the adults in the workshop are engaging in a variety of on- and off-task reactions. Now imagine that the presenter asks each participant to reflect quietly for one minute on some questions they might ask to figure out the situation. They're to discuss possible questions with a peer for three minutes, then come back as a group so that everyone can share the questions they came up with. If you were not paying attention at first—perhaps you were the one who was looking at your laptop—chances are you'll listen to your peer voice their understanding or questions, then you'll listen to the general reporting out. Or, instead of the pair activity, the presenter might draw a car and a hotel on the board, write down the two sentences ("A car pulls up to a hotel. Someone goes bankrupt"), and then add a guiding question.

The first example is a **think-pair-share** (Lyman, 1981). The second is the simple addition of visuals to represent the words spoken. Both incorporate multiple modalities: listening, speaking, and viewing.

Modalities are the various ways we learn. We read, listen, and watch, and we write, draw, speak, move, and touch. Typically, classrooms are linguistic, dominated by words rather than, say, movement or images. You are probably familiar with Howard Gardner's (1983, 2011) concept of *multiple intelligences*, which organized modalities into categories: linguistic, interpersonal, intrapersonal, visual-spatial, logical-mathematical, bodily kinesthetic, musical, and natural ways of learning. Highlighting multiple modalities helped us escape the dominance of the linguistic modality in classroom learning (Morgan, 1996).

Multiple modalities are not *learning styles*, a disproven approach that tries to match instruction to the assumed way a student learns (Pashler et al., 2008). Rather, using varied modalities, like audio and visual together, is a key to selective attention (Koelewijn et al., 2010) and to reorienting during alternating attention (Tang & Patrick, 2018). Even small visual additions, such as a combination of the teacher speaking while using visually organized print text, increase student attention (Mulqueeny et al., 2015).

The following practices are ways to enhance students' use of multiple modalities, and they reflect the ways we humans naturally learn.

Use Varied Texts

What text types do your students like to read? You may have voracious readers of print text stories, but many of your frequent video gamers and video watchers may prefer other variations of text, such as manga, comics, audiobooks, or short-form video. Varied modalities enable students to demonstrate what they've learned in different ways in their assessments, assignments, or projects. This means moving away from essays and multiple-choice tests to podcasts, videos, speeches, dance, plays, sculpture, blogs, memes, or comic strips. All use writing in some way, from drafting or designing with organizers like storyboards to final production.

Even print text varies from the traditional textbook to include bus schedules, written lyrics, emails, social media comments, and text messages (see Figure 3.3). These multiple forms of text in the context of new digital technologies can help with attention (Lankshear & Knobel, 2003) and acknowledge that learning occurs through multiple modes of communication (Albers & Harste, 2007).

FIGURE 3.3

The Multiple Forms of Texts

Varieties of Text	Examples
Print text	Trade books, magazines, bus schedules, novels, textbooks, written lyrics, poetry, journal entries, blogs, letters, emails, written speeches, written news stories, written dialogue
Print + image text	Comic strips, graphic novels, flowcharts, texts with multimedia, graphics with words, memes
Audio text	Audio speech, music, audio dialogue, podcasts
Print + audio text	Speech with transcript, music with lyrics, audiobooks with book, print text using text-to-speech
Audio + image text	Movies, short online videos, animated video shorts, audio stories with accompanying still images
Interactive text	Websites with links, social media, digital books or articles with links, discussion forums, chats, annotation tools, web design

Graphic novels are a great example of varied texts, in which the visuals and print text drive each other in the story. Graphic novels do not increase cognitive load for reading but, instead, offer a varied reading experience that promotes reading comprehension for all kinds of learners, including those with disabilities, those learning English, and those who historically have been marginalized (Aldahash & Altalhab, 2020; Cook, 2017; Hill, 2011).

Studies have shown that readers of graphic novels and comics follow a systematic approach to reading, moving back and forth among panels with faces, speech bubbles, and other print text that advances the story. These switches suggest both global attention to larger story segments and attention to story details, evidenced by readers going back to check established connections or missed details at the end of single- or double-page spreads (Mikkonen & Lautenbacher, 2019).

One way to find good graphic novels is by consulting "best of'" lists, such as *Rolling Stone*'s "50 Best Non-Superhero Graphic Novels" (Gross, 2019), NPR's list of 100 best graphic novels (Weldon & Mayer, 2017), and Goodreads's annual list of best graphic novels and comics.

It's probably not surprising that video also can help promote student attention. Tseng and colleagues (2021) attribute this attention to the *cohesion* among visual, auditory, and verbal cues in a video. They tested cohesion through viewer eye gaze and comprehension of the opening segment of the movie *The Birds*. With cohesion, the segment had bird sounds, a pet shop sign, and a woman entering a store. Researchers eliminated cohesion by removing bird sounds and blurring the indication of the type of shop. Viewer attention increased when multimodal cues were cohesive.

Multimodal cohesion also exists while simultaneously listening to an audiobook and reading it, a song while reading the lyrics, or a speech or poem while reading a copy of it. Interactive text engages both verbal and spatial abilities; we can click on links leading us through a web to connect with the main topic while drawing a concept map of the information we read on a separate sheet of paper.

Let's say you'd like to offer the graphic text format as an option for students to show their learning. First, decide on the learning goal, whether it's learning phrases in a new language or indicating steps in a science process. Then have students use an organizer for the design process, such as a storyboard to plan the product. Some good resources are Storyboardthat.com and mural.com, applications like Canva, comic creators like pixton.com, and readwritethink. org's simple comic creator for younger students.

Add Visual Organizers

Visual organizers add a visual modality to text, helping students improve selective attention and avoid distractions (Marsh et al., 2020). Researchers have tested selective attention with visual organizers, as opposed to print text, using eye tracking. They found that students moved their attention toward information in the organizer and away from text areas and then sustained their attention on the organizer (Ponce & Mayer, 2014; Wang et al., 2021). This brings attention to higher-order, significant information and helps students avoid getting distracted by irrelevant information (Rowland-Bryant et al., 2009).

The most common visual organizers align with narrative and informational text structures. These include chronological sequence, concept/definition, compare/contrast, description, generalization, episode, or process/cause/effect (Shanahan et al., 2010). Figure 3.4 provides examples of visual organizers by content and grade level.

To determine the type of organizer to use, choose the goal, such as identifying cause and effect in a text or three points in a time sequence. Then demonstrate through a think-aloud how you would use the visual organizer during the task. If students are working in pairs or groups, you'll need to clarify how the students will contribute to completing the organizer.

FIGURE 3.4

Examples of Graphic Organizers by Content and Grade

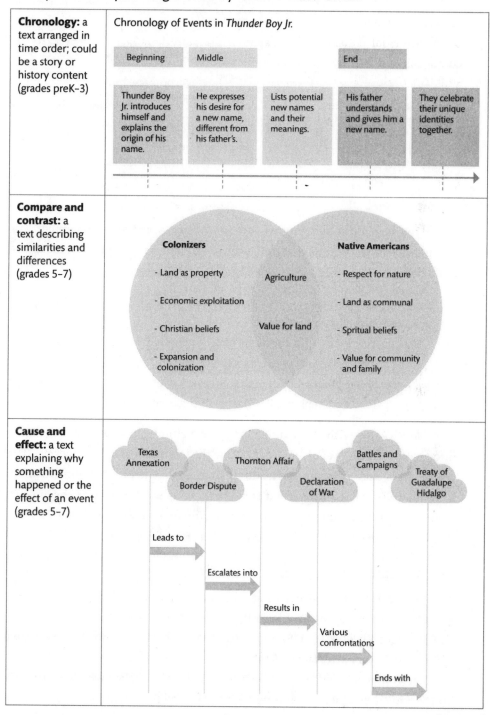

Chronology: a text arranged in time order; could be a story or history content (grades preK–3)	Chronology of Events in *Thunder Boy Jr.* Beginning Middle End Thunder Boy Jr. introduces himself and explains the origin of his name. / He expresses his desire for a new name, different from his father's. / Lists potential new names and their meanings. / His father understands and gives him a new name. / They celebrate their unique identities together.
Compare and contrast: a text describing similarities and differences (grades 5–7)	**Colonizers** / **Native Americans** - Land as property - Economic exploitation - Christian beliefs - Expansion and colonization Agriculture / Value for land - Respect for nature - Land as communal - Spritual beliefs - Value for community and family
Cause and effect: a text explaining why something happened or the effect of an event (grades 5–7)	Texas Annexation / Border Dispute / Thornton Affair / Declaration of War / Battles and Campaigns / Treaty of Guadalupe Hidalgo Leads to Escalates into Results in Various confrontations Ends with

(continued)

FIGURE 3.4 *(continued)*

Examples of Graphic Organizers by Content and Grade

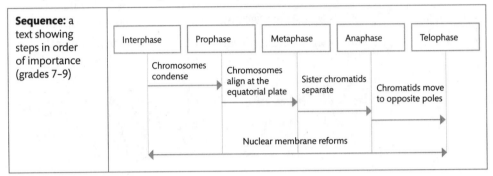

Sequence: a text showing steps in order of importance (grades 7–9)	

If you have difficulty finding the right visual organizers, remember this guiding question: What's a *visual* way to explain this topic? Consider the following:

- *A pie graph* features a circle with same or different sized slices, showing how parts make up a whole.
- *Concentric circles* with the same center point show decision-making levels or hierarchical levels in a process or system.
- *A decision tree* features lines that connect each decision point, showing options for next steps to take, based on that decision.

Using a table with rows and columns is a simple way to start organizing information. Other organizers might show the lesson's learning objectives, the agenda for a class meeting, or headings from an article or a textbook reading. They may also reflect typical text structures, such as a timeline or chronology, a Venn diagram showing similarities and differences, a problem/solution map, or a herringbone diagram showing cause and effect for a topic.

Incorporate Peer Learning

Peer learning strategies use listening and speaking modalities while interacting with others. Many peer learning strategies are based on the work of psychologist Lev Vygotsky (1978), who posited that learning is socially mediated and that voluntary attention is first social and then internalized.

Behavior specialist Ash Hall relates a story of a teacher who had come to him seeking assistance. Each time the teacher had a problem with technology and turned her back on the class to fix it, the students would erupt in talking, making it difficult for her to get them back to the lesson when she finished. Frustrated, she consulted with Ash to help with classroom inattention.

Ash provided a quick strategy: each time there was a technical problem, the teacher would give the class a prompt to discuss. If she didn't have a prompt on the tip of her tongue, she could, for example, simply ask students to share with a peer one place they'd like to go on vacation and why. The teacher tried it. Ash observed that the attention problem vanished; the students turned, talked with one another about the topic, then shifted attention back to the teacher much more quickly than when they had simply begun talking on their own.

Almost as common as this **turn and talk** is **think-pair-share** (Lyman, 1981). In think-pair-share, the teacher instructs students to think individually for a few minutes about a given topic; they can sketch or write down their initial thoughts. Next, students pair with a peer to discuss what each student thought about or wrote. Finally, the teacher asks student pairs to share what they came up with. The teacher then summarizes the activity and connects it to the next point in the lesson.

Typical small-group activities can be organized as a think-pair-share. For example, **visual synectics** (Gordon, 1961) is a strategy for synthesizing a concept learned by comparing the concept with an unrelated object or picture. In a small-group activity, peers have pictures or objects and a sentence stem; the goal is to complete the sentence. For example, "A [enter task topic] is like [the object or picture] because [their rationale for why they're alike]."

As Jamie Garcia's (2013) YouTube video shows, when her 5th grade class was studying the American Revolution, she presented the class with the stem, "The growing tension in the colonies is like [____] because [____]." One group said that the tension is like a paper clip because the colonists need to clip all the American governments together to defeat Great Britain. You could offer stems for students to choose from, which range from "[BLANK] is like Velcro" to "[BLANK] is like a Rubik's cube." Students should have some time to consider the sentence stems before joining with a peer. Thinking individually beforehand helps them alternate their attention to the peer talk and attend to the topic immediately.

As students get used to a think-pair-share routine, incorporate alternatives like the **double think-pair-share**. Students think and pair with one partner and then link with another pair. Each pair shares what they discussed, noting similarities and differences.

You may have other more structured or timed options, such as a **jigsaw** (Aronson, 1978), **numbered heads together** (Kagan, 1989), or a **three-part**

interview. In the three-part interview, four students form a team and are labeled A, B, C, and D. The teacher then poses a question to the team. In Part 1, student A interviews student B, and C interviews D. In Part 2, B interviews A, and D interviews C. Finally, in Part 3, the two pairs share. Each part can last just one minute; using one-minute timers to switch parts, students can jump into the interview and complete it before the whole-class sharing.

Introduce Intentional Movement

Around 2015, people who wore fitness trackers and smartwatches learned about a new feature called a *stand reminder*. Every 50 minutes, the device alerts the wearer to stand up. Sitting for extended periods can limit oxygen to the brain, put stress on our muscles and joints, exert pressure on our diaphragm and organs, and increase fatigue (Szczygieł, et al., 2017). If it's not a good idea for adults to be sitting for long periods, why should we expect students to do it?

Movement can help shift attention back to a task. Students are often moving in their seats or getting up, but you can develop strategies to put their movements to work in support of learning. Instead of raising hands, students can wiggle or move their legs; instead of sitting while reporting out, the group reporter can stand.

Teacher Amy Tepperman (2019) uses movement to teach fractions, as shown in her YouTube video, "Fraction in Action" from Moving EDGEucation (see www.youtube.com/watch?v=8TyC5ikOZJo). First, students get on all fours, placing hands and feet at different places on the ground. All four limbs touching the ground is one whole, she says, representing the 4/4 fraction. Next, students change their positions, with only three limbs touching the floor and holding up one arm or leg. This is 3/4. Then students practice with two limbs touching the floor—this represents 2/4—and then only one, 1/4. Then they add and subtract limbs touching the floor to add and subtract fractions. They can join with a partner to practice fractions with eight limbs, starting with all limbs touching the floor (8/8).

Researchers argue that task-relevant movements, whether full-body or arm gestures, can guide and engage attention (Mavilidi et al., 2019). Teachers can have students stand and sequence themselves in a line as events in a time-line or move their desks to create a human rendition of a cell. The **four corners** activity designates the corners of a room to represent opinions: strongly agree, agree, disagree, and strongly disagree (Bennett & Rolheiser, 2001). In reaction to a prompt, students report to the corner reflecting their views, discuss their rationale with others in their corner, and then report out.

Physical activity itself, even if unrelated to tasks, increases sustained attention (Hajar et al., 2019). If your students are continually moving in their seats or slouching in their chairs, you may discover that those behaviors feel good to them, and that's where their focus is. Introduce some easy movement breaks, such as a quick run around the room, stretches, jumping jacks, or even moving to a different spot in the room to help another student or help you with one of your tasks.

There are many movement videos on YouTube for elementary students, such as GoNoodle's (2016) three-minute video featuring Justin Timberlake's dance song "Can't Stop the Feeling" (see www.youtube.com/watch?v= KhfkYzUwYFk). There's also the Kiboomers' (2015) Freeze Dance, in which students dance, hop, skip, twirl, and dance again, all in two minutes, with a referee calling out new moves and directions to freeze in between (see www. youtube.com/watch?v=2UcZWXvgMZE). Students not only move but also learn to follow directions, good practice for alternating their attention back to academic tasks.

A more structured approach to physical activity breaks is the four-minute-a-day **FUNtervals**, shown to improve selective attention in 9- to 11-year-olds. Teachers encourage students to do whole-body movements as fast as they can for 20 seconds, with 10-second rest periods. Students jump, squat, run in place, kick, and do jumping jacks. Researchers emphasize that FUNtervals require no extra materials, no change of location, and a short time of interrupted academic activities (Ma et al., 2015).

Finally, attention researchers have shown that mindfulness meditation increases attention. Tang and Posner (2009) randomly assigned students to a brief meditation as the experimental group and to relaxation training as the control group. Each group underwent tests of attention before and after; the tests afterward showed increases in students' selective attention. The authors claim that meditation induces restful alertness, where individuals become aware of their body and mind, controlling their thoughts through gradual instructions about posture, thinking, and breathing. Examples of mindfulness activities are feeling the abdomen move while breathing, observing thoughts as though they were clouds in the sky, and moving like an animal you've imagined (Crescentini et al., 2016). Being mindful is the focus of meditation, which keeps the mind from wandering through a practice of mental stillness.

✓ Try This: Multiple Modalities

Try a brief experiment. Take a moment to stop reading, breathe in while counting to seven, hold your breath for a count of four, then breathe out for another count of seven. Where is your attention? It is probably on your breathing.

Try another. Pat your head with your left hand, and move your right hand in a circle over your stomach. Now switch movements to making circles on your head and tapping your stomach. Like breathing and counting, these intentional movements engage your attention.

If you teach fractions, you may have been moved (pun intended) by Amy Tepperman's "Fraction in Action" activity. View her how-to video at www. youtube.com/watch?v=8TyC5ikOZJo, and practice your own fractions to model for students. Or think about and model how your students might move and shift their bodies in different ways to create an image like a cell. After these movement experiments, reflect on your selective, alternating, and sustained attention.

Nurture positive relationships

Attention Principle 4: Nurture Positive Relationships

Maya Angelou is often credited with saying, "I've learned that people will forget what you said, people will forget what you did, but people will never forget how you made them feel." The childhood feelings of embarrassment, shame, or guilt described by teachers at the beginning of this chapter influenced them for years, well into their own teaching careers. The feeling that you are seen, heard, and belong also lasts a lifetime.

Teacher–student relationships long have been studied as integral to student achievement (Kincade et al., 2020). When these relationships are positive, they can help students manage their emotions, and this supports sustained attention (Babad, 1993; Danielsen et al., 2010). When there is rapport and teacher support in instruction and classroom organization (e.g., clarity of rules and proactive behavior management), students engage in fewer off-task behaviors (Vanden-broucke et al., 2018). At the other end of the spectrum, feeling excluded makes students more susceptible to attention interferences (Xu et al., 2017).

For example, if students feel positively toward their English teacher and know the teacher cares about them, they will tend to continue reading independently when asked and be more likely to resist distractions. However, if they feel a teacher dismisses them, calls them out for errors in front of other students, or invalidates their voice, they can become hyperattentive to distractors, which can promote negativity. Their minds may wander, and they may stop their independent reading (Kiat et al., 2018).

Getting to know students is essential for building student background knowledge and experiences into curriculum, as shown in Principle 2. But it's also essential for creating a positive emotional environment. Positive relationships in the classroom support the emotional regulation students need for attention to the task (Commodari, 2013; Pallini et al., 2019), as well as the sense of belonging needed for selective attention (DeWall et al., 2009; Xu et al., 2017). The strategies that follow are about creating positive relationships, from acknowledging students and building relationships throughout the year, to clear communication and a shared voice in the classroom.

Say Student Names Often

Danny Vương, a 4th and 5th grade teacher, decided to be a model. In his first years of teaching, he went by "Mr. Vong" because it was easier for staff and students to pronounce. Even though his name is only five letters long, it had been mispronounced and frequently misspelled as he grew up. As he noted, "I realized it was hypocritical of me to value every student's name, but not value my own." So Danny decided to use the correct pronunciation and spelling of his last name, Vương (pronounced V-ugh-ng). Danny shared with his students both the pronunciation and the origin of his name (he was named after a Vietnamese king, Vua Hùng Vương). Initially, his 4th graders called him "Mr. Vong," but when they became 5th graders, they got used to calling him Mr. Vương. It was worth it, he said, "for kids to believe that their own name has value. We have to model it ourselves with our own names."

The importance of learning and saying student names correctly seems obvious. If someone repeatedly says your name incorrectly, do you feel seen? Heard? Students of color often encounter mispronunciations, and this can have a lasting negative effect on their self-perception and worldview, inhibiting the positive relationships you're trying to build (Kohli & Solórzano, 2012).

Those who are ethnic minorities in the United States also experience negative reactions from others if they decide to adopt Anglo-sounding names (Zhao & Biernat, 2018).

Knowing students' names is the first step in learning who students are, and it conveys that you care about them. Even just greeting students by name and saying something positive at the beginning of class can increase on-task behavior by 27 percent (Allday & Pakurar, 2007). Asking student names, adding student photos to attendance lists or a bulletin board, or asking them to introduce themselves to the class help students feel seen, while giving teachers multiple ways to learn, practice, and **use names consistently**.

Share Decision Making

Middle school teacher Barb Miller uses voting to develop classroom norms. Students typically brainstorm about 10 rules, and Barb lists them on a large poster paper. Then students vote by placing stickers next to their top three choices. The five rules that get the most stickers become the norms for the class. Throughout the year, Barb revisits the norms, asking students where the norms are working, where they might improve, and whether the decided-on norms need to be revisited.

Shared decision-making strategies build trust, respect, and cooperation in classrooms (Butler & Rothstein, 1988). In the world of work, decisions are made in a variety of ways: by command, through consultation or consensus, and by voting (Grenny et al., 2022). In a classroom, command is typical; the teacher makes the decision and tells the students what it is. But some teachers incorporate other forms of decision making. They may use voting for classroom rules, like Barb did, or involve students in low-stakes decisions, such as asking the class if they want to start a new topic or stay with the current one.

Consensus is collective decision making. Barb's class voted on the top five rules. But another option is asking for a student proposal, such as, "I propose that the five rules that we came up with as a class today are the rules for the next quarter." Then, for consensus, students might use **fist to five** (Fletcher, 2002), a strategy in which students hold up their fist or some or all of their fingers (see Figure 3.5). One or two fingers signal low agreement; three or more signal higher agreement.

Let's see how the teacher models this with our voting example.

> Teacher: I propose that we adopt these five rules for our class through December and then revisit them at that point. Fist to five.

Students all raise their hands with three, four, and five fingers. The teacher holds up two fingers.

Teacher: I held up two fingers, which means that I minimally support the proposal and want more discussion. So now I'm responsible for telling you what I want to talk about. Ready?

Students nod.

Teacher: Rule 3 says, "Respect one another." I like the idea and heard some of you talk about it on our original list. But should we define it?

Student A: Respect means that we say kind things.

Student B: And don't put people down.

Student C: It is about listening and shutting up.

After further discussion, the teacher proposes that the respect rule should have two meanings: "say kind words" and "listen without interrupting." She asks the class if they accept having those two meanings written next to the rule, or whether they want the two meanings to appear as two separate rules. The students start discussing this; after a minute, the teacher stops them.

FIGURE 3.5
Fist to Five Consensus Decision-Making Strategy

Hand Indicator	**Level of Agreement** Fist, 1, or 2 fingers raised means further discussion is needed; 3, 4, or 5 fingers raised means the proposal passes without further discussion.
Raise a fist	I do not support the proposal, and therefore I block it. I need to talk more about the proposal. It will need to be changed for me to be comfortable with it.
Raise 1 finger	I do not support the proposal, but I won't block it. I have strong reservations and need to discuss possible changes.
Raise 2 fingers	I have minimal support for the proposal. I would like to discuss minor issues for potential adjustments.
Raise 3 fingers	I am neutral about this proposal. I am not in total agreement, but I am comfortable enough for the proposal to pass without further discussion.
Raise 4 fingers	I support the proposal solidly. I think the proposal is a good idea.
Raise all 5 fingers	I support the proposal solidly. I think the proposal is a great idea, and I will do what I can to promote it.

Teacher: Let's check with a proposal. Anyone can state the new proposal at this point, but because I started this, I will state it. I propose that we have these five rules as everyone agreed until December, but that we should add "say kind words" and "listen without interrupting" next to the respect rule.

Students throw up their hands. The teacher sees two threes and two twos.

Teacher: OK, Mirna or Sam, you are the twos. Please state your perspective.

Mirna: The respect rule should be split in two instead of having two meanings.

Other students pipe up, and Sam nods his head. The teacher sees this and then asks Mirna to offer a new proposal with the revision. The teacher asks for fist to five again. When all students raise at least three fingers, consensus is achieved.

Using **voting** or fist to five for rules at the beginning of the year lays the groundwork for their use throughout the year. Voting works better with larger groups and fist to five with smaller groups. In the example of establishing norms, students could vote first, then use fist to five for the final discussion, or the teacher could facilitate a discussion, list rules, then use fist to five for the final choice.

Either way, the practice is useful. When students come to a consensus about rules, they've thought about how those rules apply to them, which promotes cooperative, on-task behavior and awareness of the role they play as part of the community (Palomares et al., 2014). It's also useful for getting to the bottom of some attention issues. For example, a teacher notices that many students aren't paying attention. Is this because the students don't understand the task—or because they don't agree with it? The teacher can either make a proposal or ask for a proposal to find a solution for the off-task behaviors. Sharing decision making means that community development has begun.

Improve Relationships Throughout the Year

High school teacher Sean Miller says that relationship building never stops. He takes opportunities to get to know students while they are off task. When students are looking at something on their phone or talking about a song, he asks, "What intrigues you about that?" Or, when students are doodling or drawing, he asks, "Would you be open to telling me about your drawing?" Sean notices these behaviors as he walks around the room, so there's a degree of informality about it. Students have come to him after class to continue talking about their interest, something that's not likely to happen if he simply tells them to stop the off-task behavior.

Cultivating relationships throughout the year helps with making curricular connections as you continue to learn more about students. But intentional and more focused communication helps students feel they belong. Some teachers make a **positive phone call home** to every family throughout the year, which may take most of the year to complete! Or they use the **two by ten** strategy of talking with one student two minutes a day, 10 days in a row (Gragg & Collet, 2023; McKibben, 2014).

Third grade teacher Kyle Schwartz once wrote on the whiteboard in the classroom, "I wish my teacher knew…" and asked her students to fill in the blank on a notecard and give her the notecard. She compiled the responses in her book, *I Wish My Teacher Knew: How One Question Can Change Everything* (2016). Nycole Bradshaw tried the question for the first time when she was a student teacher in her mentor teacher Emmy's classroom. Emmy's approach, Nycole relates, was to "build relationships from day one." Emmy talked to students about her weekends, shared pictures, and encouraged students to show their photos, too. She talked about how her family came to the United States from Japan, something highly relevant to the many students who were refugees. Together, Nycole and Emmy implemented "I wish my teacher knew…" a few weeks into getting to know students.

Many answers stood out to Nycole. "I wish my teacher knew…"

- That my father was an alcoholic, and he yells at me all the time.
- That when I'm really sleepy, it's because I live in a loud neighborhood.
- That I really do like school, but I don't want to be made fun of because of it.
- That sometimes I answer wrong on purpose because I don't want people to know that I'm smart or paying attention in class.

Emmy challenged Nycole, saying, "What if *you* were the lead teacher? How would you respond to these notes?" As Nycole discovered, the follow-ups to these messages are necessary and varied, something she now does in her own classroom. Follow-ups include problem solving conflicts; discussing interests; asking permission to connect students with a counselor; or asking other questions, such as, "How would you like me to support you in class?" "Do you want to check in with me about this again next week?" or "How do you think this affects your attention in class?" Alternatively, when students share something they like, you can incorporate it into course content and further conversations.

Some teachers may not like or be ready for the classroom trust and processes needed to encourage student sharing in these ways. Teachers have suggested changes to redirect this prompt, from "I wish my teacher knew..." to "I wish my teacher would..." to focus on possible actions teachers can take to help students pay attention (see Venet, 2021).

Set Up Communication Frames

Teacher Lindsay Cesari noticed that her 9th grade students were good at offering opinions or ideas in academic conversations, but not at building on others' ideas to continue a conversation thread. To help students with this concept, she models using LEGO blocks in class. The first time she did this, she started with the prompt "Valentine's Day is the best holiday ever." Here's what ensued.

> Student 1: I love Valentine's Day because I get to show my friends how much I like them.
>
> Teacher puts a LEGO block down.
>
> Student 2: Yeah! I did that for my friends. I bought my friends lollipops this year.
>
> Teacher places a second block on the first one, building a tower.
>
> Student 3: One of my friends left me a carnation in my locker.
>
> Teacher adds a third block.
>
> Student 4: That's stupid. I hate Valentine's Day because it is just spending money, and I don't have money to start with.
>
> Teacher points out that they are starting a new thread in the conversation, and she places a block beside the other three.
>
> Student 5: Valentine's Day is so much pressure. I feel like I have to show people I care about them, and I don't want to do that.
>
> Teacher places another block to show that they are starting a second tower.

After modeling, students sit in groups and repeat this process, using sentence stems for a taller tower when they are building on a conversation and different stems to start another tower when they switch to a new thread in the conversation. Lindsay listens to their meta-conversation about where to put their LEGO blocks, and she watches groups to see if they're placing them appropriately. She may also challenge them in terms of time and give a new instruction: "In the next two minutes, build either three new towers or a conversation that's at least five blocks tall."

Lindsay used **a communication frame** for academic conversations called *building on ideas* (Zwiers & Crawford, 2009). Other communication frames are *elaborating and clarifying, supporting ideas with examples, applying and connecting,* and *paraphrasing and summarizing* (Zwiers & Crawford, 2009) (see Figure 3.6.)

FIGURE 3.6
Sample Prompts

Communication Frame	Question Samples	Student Response Samples
Elaborate and clarify	Can you elaborate? What do you mean by...? Can you tell me more about...? What makes you think that?	I think it means that... In other words...
Support ideas with examples	Can you give an example? Can you show me where it says that? Can you be more specific? Are there any cases of that?	For example... In the text, it said that... One case showed that...
Build on or challenge another's ideas	What do you think? Can you add to this idea? Do you agree? What might be other points of view?	I would add that... Then again, I think that... I want to expand on your point about...
Apply and connect	How can we apply this idea in our lives? What can we learn from this character/party/story? If you were...	In my life... I think it can teach us... If I were..., I would have...
Paraphrase and summarize	What have we discussed so far? How should we summarize what we talked about?	We can say that... The main theme/point of the text seems to be...

Source: Adapted from "How to Start Academic Conversations," by J. Zwiers & M. Crawford, 2009, *Educational Leadership, 66*(7), 70–73.

Each frame uses guiding questions, such as, "What do you think?" "Can you add to this idea?" "Do you agree?" and "What might be other points of view?" Frames also employ prompts for student responses, such as, "I would add that...," "Then again, I think that...," and "I want to build on your point about...."

Conversation builds relationships. Now when Lindsay says, "Build on that idea," students listen to one another, attend to the topic, and build ideas through conversation.

Teach self-regulation

Attention Principle 5: Teach Self-Regulation

As adults, we can notice our negative *thoughts* and shift them to positive. We can go from "I didn't do well on that work task" to "I started the task, got feedback, and now I can attend to the task again and keep going." If we identify a *feeling* of fear or sadness, we can sit with the feeling or write about it to move to a more pleasant feeling and refocus on a task. We can also recognize our *behaviors* and change those, too. For example, I keep picking up my phone instead of working. To stop the attention interruption, I put my phone in the next room and refocus on work.

Self-regulation is effectively monitoring and adjusting our thoughts, feelings, and behaviors. When we are effective self-regulators, we can control our inner processes, such as maintaining attention (Vohs & Baumeister, 2016). Self-regulation is voluntary and goal-directed, such as when I intend to and *do* ignore distractions while reading or when I intend to and *do* sustain focus on the reading for the next 10 minutes. In fact, both self-regulation and effortful attention occur in similar brain areas responsible for goal-oriented thinking (Posner & Rothbart, 2009; Rueda, Posner et al., 2004).

Self-regulation is perhaps the most challenging of the five principles for promoting attention. Do you think about how you notice and monitor—or fail to notice and monitor—your own thoughts, feelings, and behaviors every day? As adults, we still can obsess about something we said, feel angry for longer than we would like, and compulsively grab our phones. Self-regulation is not easy, regardless of how much practice we've had. So, for children and adolescents with developing brains and less life experience, why would we complain about *their* lack of self-regulation? We often tend to ask ourselves, "Why can't students plan their time and organize their materials? Why are they off task or not completing assignments when I provided the instructions?"

Teaching self-regulation requires taking steps. Unlike the other principles, which are about providing structures and opportunities for student attention, self-regulation is about the gradual shift of responsibility to the student. The teacher models, then works with, and finally supports students as they learn to regulate themselves (Pearson & Gallagher, 1983). All of the following strategies include some form of modeling and working with students on self-regulation so they can ultimately monitor themselves.

Show How to Recognize Behaviors, Feelings, and Thoughts

Fourth grade teacher Adrienne Hayes asks students at the beginning of the year, "What does being on task look like?" She listens to student responses and then summarizes that it looks like reading, writing, and talking in pursuit of a class goal. Adrienne tells students, "If it looks like you are not on task, I want you to ask yourself, 'Am I on task?' Then I want you to decide from there. I work from what I see, so I want *you* to check your behavior first, and then I will check in with you."

Adrienne is showing students how to recognize their behavior by defining the behavior, having them ask themselves about their own behavior, and then describing the role she'll play in supporting them. As the school year progresses and she sees a student walking around the room when they should be working on a task, she'll ask them privately, "Did you check in with yourself?" The student will say yes or no, and then they'll talk about what it looks and feels like to be on task.

Danny Vuong demonstrates self-awareness of feelings to his 4th and 5th graders by using a mood meter, a tool developed in 2005 by Marc Brackett, founding director of the Yale Center for Emotional Intelligence. A **mood meter** is based on two dimensions of feeling: levels of pleasantness and levels of energy (Posner et al., 2005). Danny displays a four-quadrant graph on his bulletin board for student reference: the Y axis points to high energy above the X axis and low energy below the X axis; the X axis is pleasant on the right side of the Y axis and unpleasant on the left side of the Y axis. Each quadrant has a color: red for unpleasant high energy; yellow for pleasant high energy; green for pleasant low energy, and blue for unpleasant low energy.

At the beginning of the year, Danny brainstorms with his students about what thoughts or actions would fall in each quadrant. Here are some examples students provided:

- Unpleasant high-energy quadrant: "When I feel unprepared"; "Injustice"

- Pleasant high-energy quadrant: "Students are kind to one another"; "When I feel understood"
- Unpleasant low-energy quadrant: "I don't get enough sleep"; "When I sense other people are sad"
- Pleasant low-energy quadrant: "Feeling organized"; "Listening to calm music"

Danny then practices with his students by modeling his current feelings, asks students about theirs, and facilitates a discussion about situations during the day when they might notice moving from one quadrant to another.

Adrienne and Danny focused on helping students recognize *behaviors* and *emotions*. Now, what about self-awareness of *thinking*? You can use a thinking task, such as reading, to help students become aware of their own thoughts. As we read, our minds will wander in places. Show students that when this happens, they should notice the wandering and put a dot or star in the sentence where they stopped, start reading again, and repeat the process. After a few times, they can stop to reflect: Did I stop because a certain thought drew me away? Because I heard a noise? Because I didn't understand the reading?

You may recognize awareness of thinking as *metacognition*. In 1979, John Flavell described metacognition as the awareness of self, task, strategy, and performance. Self-regulation brings behaviors and emotions into the mix but uses the same basic steps of first becoming aware, choosing what to do next, trying that strategy, and then reflecting on the strategy to adjust it.

The sections that follow describe strategies to teach students after they learn to become aware of their behaviors, feelings, and thoughts.

Set Up Self-Regulation Strategies When the Year Begins

Adrienne's discussions with her students focused on one thing: student awareness of their on- or off-task behavior and how they could check with themselves to redirect their behavior. **Self-talk** ("Am I on task?") is one strategy for redirecting students to a task ("What task am I supposed to be doing right now?"). If the student is unsure of the task, it's also a strategy for asking for teacher support (e.g., using a signal to let the teacher know support is needed or asking a question for help). These self-talk and teacher communication strategies become basic behavior regulation techniques to build on throughout the year.

Danny brainstorms emotional self-regulation strategies with students, such as taking deep breaths, talking about the situation, listening to music, doing puzzles, and engaging in self-talk and positive affirmations. One self-regulation strategy is the **peace corner** (Lantieri, 2008). Danny used two filing cabinets to block off the space. Then he added a fuzzy carpet; a pillow; inspirational posters; a mirror on which he wrote, "You are in control"; notepads for drawing; and an expandable breathing ball. He also included My Calm Place cards (Neiman et al., 2015), which illustrate regulation strategies. In the **starfish strategy**, for example, the student stands tall with arms up and legs out to make an X, then reaches higher with the right hand and pushes down with the left foot, then repeats on the other side to imitate a starfish.

Teaching students how to use the peace corner starts with the "why" behind emotional regulation, so they know that the peace corner is not a place to play. During the first two weeks of school, Danny has every student try out the peace corner for five minutes. The goal is to rejoin the class in a peaceful and calm manner. If he observes that a student is there for more than five minutes, that their mood meter does not reflect why they are there, and that their demeanor is still unregulated, then the two of them talk. Danny says, "I see you were in the peace corner for more than five minutes. I want to check in with you to see how you are." He asks if something is bothering them. If the answer is no, then he reteaches how to use the peace corner. Overall, Danny notices that when students use the corner and return calmly to their seats, they alternate their attention more quickly to the task and focus.

Some teachers model various strategies for emotional regulation. Here's a list of five to start. Take time to review them, model them with the class, have students practice them as a group, and then add student ideas to the list.

- Breathe in for a count of seven, hold the breath for a count of four, then breathe out for a count of eight.
- Count backward slowly from 10.
- Write in your journal for one minute.
- Squeeze your stress ball.
- Tighten and relax all your muscles.

The strategies that follow are behavioral, emotional, cognitive, or all three. The focus is on developing structures that teachers demonstrate, practice with students, and then have students use themselves so they're able to select, alternate, and sustain their attention while moving through tasks.

Use Checklists Consistently

In the early 2000s, a research team implemented a 19-item team communication checklist for surgeons in eight hospitals in eight cities around the world, from Seattle, Washington, to Ifakara, Tanzania (Haynes et al., 2009). The result was a 36 percent reduction in complications across 3,733 non-cardiac-surgery patients. Airline pilots, too, have long used checklists. Routine checklist use was a major factor in the heroism of Captain Chesley Sullenberger and his copilot in their successful landing of U.S. Airways Flight 1549 in the Hudson River in 2009. It took them 3 minutes and 28 seconds to identify that both engines were disabled by birds, determine that the river was the only place to land, and land safely in the water.

Checklists are a key tool for selective and sustained attention among surgeons and pilots, despite their extensive experience repeating the same procedures. We also use checklists every day to regulate our own behaviors, such as when assembling furniture, tracking student assignments, and staying on task while shopping.

If you notice your students talking and looking around the room when you're modeling long division on the board, you can give them a bulleted list of steps for the procedure and model how to use it. When students stop or make a mistake, they can alternate their attention to the checklist to find out where they were, ask a question, or return to the task.

Reading strategies are an easy way to get started with checklists because they have been shown to increase selective attention for both native English speakers and students learning English (Prichard & Atkins, 2019; Stevens et al., 2013). A popular strategy is SQ3R (Robinson, 1941). A reader Surveys (S) the reading before reading the selection; develops Questions (Q) about the reading; and then Reads the text (R), Recites the text (R), and Reviews the reading (R). SQ3R has shown promise in both elementary and secondary grades, but it isn't for everyone. A student may wonder, "What exactly does *survey* mean?" If they perceive the survey step as unclear, a student may discard the strategy as not useful from the start.

FLIP (Allen, 2008) may be a more concrete and accessible approach. The reader Flips (F) through the reading to look for organization, interest, writing style, or background knowledge; Looks (L) at the visuals to see what they can learn from them or how the visuals relate to the headings; Informs (I) themself about topics in the reading from headings, paragraphs, or margins; and Predicts (P) what they think the reading will be about and what challenges it might offer.

Note taking also features concrete steps. AVID (Advancement Via Individual Determination) (Swanson, 1989, 2004) has an acronym to help with note taking called STAR. The student Sets up the paper (adds the title, draws the lines for a Cornell-style paper setup); Takes notes (adds details or drawings);

Adds to the notes (adds questions or overlooked details, uses different fonts or colors); and Reviews the notes (adds summaries, talks with a peer, draws connective lines).

To create a checklist, start with the goal. If you want students to solve a math problem, here are some steps:

1. Read and annotate the problem.
2. Choose a strategy to solve the problem.
3. Carry out the strategy.
4. Check the solution.

If you want students to plan one of two possible field trips, steps might include the following:

1. Review the two options.
2. Circle what interests you about the option you prefer.
3. Write one downside of that option in the margin.
4. At the end of the option, write a sentence that starts with the prompt, "We students will learn [BLANK], which will connect to [this topic] that we have been studying."

If your students are planning to create a comic strip with a partner, steps might include the following:

1. Choose two formats to use for the final strip.
2. Write down two options for the story topic.
3. Choose one topic, and enter four events in the story on the story map.
4. Stop and check with your partner.

Once you model how to use the checklist, work with students as they see how tasks are broken down, and encourage them to adapt the checklist to their needs. After practicing and with your help, they will start making checklists themselves.

Give Task-Specific Feedback

What are the differences among these three statements?

Teacher A: Good job! Keep working.

Teacher B: Numbers 1 through 5 are wrong; you need to redo them correctly.

Teacher C: I see you've completed step 1 of 3, with the definition of light as energy that we can see. I see the examples are empty. What's an example of energy that we can see?

It's not difficult to see the difference. Statements A and B are not feedback; they're a judgment of the work (good, wrong) and a behavior command. Statement C *is* feedback—it includes the goal (three steps), what the student did already (Step 1), and guidance for where to go next (write examples of energy). Depending on the student's answer to the teacher's question, the teacher could provide an example (candles, sun, fire) or suggest a place where the student can go to find the answer.

This **three-step feedback** is specific to a task; it includes a goal, how the steps work toward the goal, and guidance for the next step. Meta-analyses show that feedback has a large effect on student achievement (Hattie & Timperley, 2007) and on directing attention to the task at hand (Kruger & DeNisi, 1996; Wisniewski et al., 2020).

In Chapter 2, I described a student whose mind appeared to be wandering during an on-screen reading task. The teacher followed the three feedback steps. First, she affirmed what the student already knew and had done in the reading. Second, she modeled reading the heading aloud and wondering aloud what strategies to choose to keep going with the reading, ending with a suggestion to break down the information. Third, she invited the student to draw four boxes on a piece of paper, and they agreed that the student would use each box to document one takeaway from each of the first three paragraphs. This last step enabled student self-regulation: the student and teacher created the boxes together and reached agreement, then the teacher focused the student's attention on the first paragraph and on documenting a takeaway in the first box as the next concrete step. After the feedback steps, the student knew the teacher would check back with them soon, offering more support for self-regulating.

You can start practicing feedback by keeping in mind the three steps of this approach—specifying a goal, how the steps work toward that goal, and guidance for the next step—when checking on individual students. Or you can review student work for the three steps: what they got right, what the pattern is for mistakes, and what could be a next-step suggestion for the student. For example, on a math worksheet, you notice that the student adds the first column correctly, but the next column shows errors. You see that mistakes occur because the student didn't align the columns correctly. As the third step, you would guide them on drawing vertical lines on the paper.

Feedback has been described as self-regulation that enables students to monitor their own attention by building from what they did well and from the guidance provided for next steps, then monitoring and adjusting their progress and performance (Butler & Winne, 1995). Other self-regulation strategies can use the same process. For example, create a graphic organizer that lists a success, a new goal, and checkboxes with milestones toward the goal.

✓ Try This: Nurture Positive Relationships and Teach Self-Regulation

This first experiment addresses your ability to recall people's names, something we focused on in our discussion of Principle 4 (nurture positive relationships), when we noted the importance of using student names. Think about adults whose names consistently escape your mind. Select a person whose name you typically don't remember at work. Practice associating their name with something concrete in your mind that only you will remember. Consider Jim Kwik's acronym SUAVE (see www.youtube.com/shorts/R-qFpc_pzql); you Say the name, Use it, Ask about it, Visualize it, and End with it. Test yourself by greeting this person and using their name five days in a row. Then try this with five new students. Reflect on how saying names focused your own attention, as well as the attention of those you addressed.

This second experiment addresses emotion management, a central point of Principle 5 (teach self-regulation). Think about a situation at home or work that feels challenging to you. Write it down, and then take a moment to let yourself *feel*. Then observe the emotion. What is it? Are you angry (annoyed, offended, frustrated); sad (mournful, pessimistic, disappointed); anxious (afraid, confused, stressed); hurt (isolated, abandoned, aggrieved); or embarrassed (ashamed, self-conscious, guilty)? Reflect on how the feeling changes from, say, stressed to happy (confident, relieved, relaxed) because you learned something new that will bring you better results the next time around. How can you use this experience to model for students to help with attention?

Conclusion

Children are frequently off task. It's part of their developmental path. As they mature into adolescence and adulthood, their ability to regulate attention matures (Godwin et al., 2013; Luna, 2009; Posner & Rothbart, 2007). Cumulative experiences also influence attention. We tend to pay attention to what we have experienced as success and have received feedback on in the past. For example, when chunking reading, connections to personal background knowledge, previously learned concepts, positive interactions with teachers, and setting personal goals and monitoring associated strategies all contribute to focusing attention on new, similar tasks (Awh et al., 2012).

The five principles discussed in this chapter do not map precisely onto the root causes of inattention we discovered from our assessments in Chapter 2. But they do address them. As you find root causes, match strategies to the causes, then continue to assess and adjust the strategies, you will continuously improve the conditions for attention in your classroom.

You may also have students who seem to have ongoing inattention or impulsivity issues. These strategies can help those students, too, but you also wonder about the common diagnosis associated with chronic attention issues: attention deficit hyperactivity disorder, or ADHD. The next chapter describes what ADHD is and is not, and how to help those particular students with more targeted strategies.

Chapter Reflection: Rate Your Practice

Reflect on the five principles for promoting attention and associated strategies by recalling what you currently do and what you'd like to try. Rate your current use of strategies as 1, 2, 3, 4, or 5, with 5 being highest.

1. Strategies for reducing cognitive load—the amount of information in working memory—will help students attend to the concepts and work through the tasks. How would you rate your current use of strategies to **reduce cognitive load:** 1, 2, 3, 4, or 5? Why did you select that rating?

2. Incorporating student background knowledge into content will encourage students to attend to what they find relevant about the task. How would you rate your current use of strategies to **incorporate students' background knowledge:** 1, 2, 3, 4, or 5? Why did you select that rating?

3. Introducing multiple modes of engagement can enable students to attend and learn in a variety of ways. How would you rate your current

use of strategies to **integrate multiple modalities:** 1, 2, 3, 4, or 5? Why did you select that rating?

4. Building positive relationships throughout the year will encourage attention by fostering students' sense of belonging. How would you rate your current use of strategies to **nurture positive relationships:** 1, 2, 3, 4, or 5? Why did you select that rating?

5. Teaching students skills for self-regulation can enable them to monitor—and self-correct—their own attention voluntarily. How would you rate your current use of strategies to **teach self-regulation:** 1, 2, 3, 4, or 5? Why did you select that rating?

Review each of your answers. Which strategies would you like to adapt or try in an area where you rated the lowest? In an area where you rated the highest?

📚 Learn More: Principles for Promoting Attention and Their Strategies

The principles for promoting attention presented in this chapter derive from attention research. However, these concepts are probably not new to you. In fact, although I describe how they relate to attention research in each section, you may recognize their presence in literacy education and approaches to teaching and learning like culturally responsive pedagogies, competency-based education, and both problem-based and project-based learning.

This is because, since the 1980s, education researchers have increasingly used what we know about learning from psychology, sociology, and neuroscience to shift the philosophy of school from teacher-centered to student-centered. Therefore, all these strategies are centered on learning and on the student as the learner.

Now, no matter the education theory or practice, the science of learning has become integrative. Darling-Hammond and colleagues (2020) provide a framework of a supportive environment, system of supports, productive instructional strategies, and social-emotional development. We know that, conceptually, these practices help students learn. Yet, like research on the brain networks of attention (Posner et al., 2016), the connections are complex. In this book, we explored what led to the current complexity of the research—a cognitive perspective of attention alongside three types of attention (selective, alternating, and sustained). Therefore, a place to build knowledge of integrative learning perspectives might be within the initial learning theories themselves.

In your ongoing learning about the principles for promoting attention and their strategies, I suggest building a foundation on what you already know. Three categories of learning theories are behaviorism, cognitivism, and constructivism. The first two are referenced in these first three chapters, and the third, constructivism, is where knowledge is created by adapting new information with previous knowledge and experience—specifically, Principle 2. You learned about constructivism in your foundations of education course. John Dewey said that education should center around a child's experience in a democratic community. Lev Vygotsky continued, saying a student learns based on their culture and social interactions with others. Vygotsky's zone of proximal development is the space where a student learns with a more knowledgeable other, a central concept involved with the scaffolding in Principle 5, teaching self-regulation.

From here, seek out models of instructional design and asset-based teaching that build on these concepts. But, like any of "today's" theories and perspectives in education, they didn't begin in the 20th century. The Aztecs in the 1300s learned through apprenticeships. The Greek philosophers taught us how to ask questions from multiple perspectives. Indigenous worldviews are of the whole person and how we live and learn in relationships with others.

The future is upon us, and it bridges original philosophies with the knowledge base of learning over the past half century. As Darling-Hammond and colleagues (2020) summarize, this knowledge base can move us from the "factory-model conceptions of organizations that privileged standardization and minimized relationships" in the mid-1900s to

> organiz[ing] around developmentally-supportive relationships; coherent and well-integrated approaches to supports, including home and school connections; well-scaffolded instruction that intentionally supports the development of social, emotional, and academic skills, habits, and mindsets; and culturally competent, personalized responses to the assets and needs that each individual child presents. (p. 133)

The principles for promoting attention can help guide us into a system of integrated, learning-centered education.

4

Addressing ADHD:
A Special Challenge for Attention

In one of the most-watched TED Talks, *Do Schools Kill Creativity?*, the late Sir Ken Robinson (2006) relates the story of Gillian Lynne, choreographer of the musicals *Cats* and *Phantom of the Opera*. In the 1930s, Gillian's parents received a letter from her school noting that she was inattentive and fidgety. Her mother took Gillian to a therapist. In the therapist's office, the therapist got up from the desk, turned the radio on, told Gillian they would be right back, and left the office with her mother to watch her from the window.

They saw Gillian get up from the couch and start moving to the music. It was then that the therapist told her mother, "Gillian isn't sick. She's a dancer." Her mother enrolled her in dance school, which Gillian described as "filled with people like me. People who couldn't sit still. People who had to move to think." Robinson concludes,

> [Gillian] couldn't concentrate. She's fidgeting. I think now they would say she has ADHD. Wouldn't you? But this was the 1930s, and ADHD hadn't been invented at this point. It wasn't an available condition [he laughs, scattered audience laughs]. People weren't aware that they could have that. Today, someone else might have put her on medication and told her to calm down.

The laughs from Robinson and the audience about the later invention of attention deficit hyperactivity disorder (ADHD) acknowledge a specific educational perspective. In the 1930s, schools were—and arguably remain—set up to expect students to sit still at a desk and value such strengths as verbal abilities

95

(Gardner, 1983, 2011). But more than a half century of research on how people learn now refutes the efficacy of relying predominantly on verbal abilities in static, sit-and-get classrooms (National Academies of Sciences, Engineering, and Medicine, 2018). Our system is slow to change; what now might be called ADHD-like behavior, like Gillian's propensity to move, still does not fit into the system.

This is not to make light of an ADHD diagnosis—or claim it's wrong. Gillian's story simply demonstrates that our education system does not always accommodate students' individual differences well or constructively. Our system has prohibited education for many—Black Americans during and after slavery and segregation; Indigenous peoples, who were relegated to special boarding schools in the 20th century; and, until the 1970s, people with disabilities. This has led to continued exclusion for these groups today.

Despite John Dewey's push for progressive education, which considered individual learner interests and needs, standardization and behaviorism took hold in the 1900s. This imposed a one-size-fits-all approach, which Paulo Freire (1970) called a "banking system," where students sit and listen passively to a teacher depositing knowledge. This model still remains, despite the efforts of contemporary teachers and other education reformers to place learning and students at the center of schooling.

Our students differ from one another—and some have severe attention and impulsivity issues that can challenge the adults around them at home and school. Because we're all human, teachers can carry unconscious biases about such issues and inadvertently behave in ways that ignore, or even hurt, students. The good news is that the more reflective and self-corrective we are, the more skilled we become in understanding our own biases and devising strategies to overcome them to enable all of our students to learn well.

To that end, teachers should realize that an ADHD diagnosis can help both them and their students. It can unlock valuable resources for students whose strengths may not fit the demands of the academic environment and whose inattentive or impulsive behaviors may adversely affect their success in school (Pérez-Álvarez, 2017). It also can alert teachers to provide more individualized assistance to these students.

Some of the material that follows is fairly technical. The intent is not to make the reader an expert on ADHD. Rather, the intent is practical: to alert teachers to strategies for promoting attention that can help students with ADHD.

Understanding ADHD—what it is and is not—is important for teachers because they are at the forefront of addressing ADHD issues in schools (Sax &

Kautz, 2003). And ADHD diagnoses are pervasive. It is one of the most common childhood diagnoses, with approximately 10 to 11 percent of students receiving that diagnosis. These figures have grown rapidly in recent years; between 2003 and 2011, there was a 42 percent increase in ADHD diagnoses, from 7.8 to 11 percent (NIMH, 2019). A National Health Interview survey showed similar increases, from 6.1 percent in 1997 to 10.2 percent in 2016 (Xu et al., 2018), and a 2024 study showed a continued increase from 2016 to 2022, citing an 11.4 percent incidence rate (Danielson et al., 2024).

These increases don't mean that ADHD is more *prevalent*. There is no evidence that children have more attention issues now than in the past, but clinicians increasingly are recognizing these difficulties, and there is increased public awareness (Danielson et al., 2014; Faraone et al., 2021). Even with increased recognition, however, misdiagnoses are still a problem. Students who are youngest in their class and those with milder symptoms or who have not been comprehensively evaluated make up significant proportions of the recent increases, as do children from historically marginalized racial and ethnic groups, who are often labeled as having disruptive behavior disorders instead (Fadus et al., 2020; Kazda et al., 2021; Visser et al., 2014). This emphasizes the importance of correctly identifying and supporting students early on (Ayano et al., 2023).

This chapter will encourage informed conversations about ADHD by explaining what it is, how referrals for evaluation work, and how we diagnose ADHD and classify students. It also examines the issue of medication and outlines principles for promoting attention for students with persistent attention challenges.

Does This Student Have ADHD?

Third grade teacher Nycole Bradshaw tells the story of an 8-year-old boy who, when the class transitioned from sitting at their desks to sitting on the carpet, would "take the scenic route," winding among the desks and running around the room. Nycole first focused on safety; he could run into another student. She moved his desk far from the carpet so that he had a specific running route that was clear of other students. The route also offered the space and time for him to imagine a run on a baseball field; in his mind, the carpet was home plate for him to slide into at the end of his run. Nycole also noticed that the student frequently moved in his seat. Because his desk was next to a wall, she invited him to stand and work instead. "He is not going to pay attention if he is focused on sitting there, uncomfortable," Nycole reflected.

Did Nycole's student have ADHD? Nycole assessed his off-task behaviors: the student ran during a class transition and often squirmed in his seat. To Nycole, these were sensory functions, so she created conditions that involved movement, which improved the student's attention. These strategies worked so well that when she discovered another student who paid more attention while walking back and forth, making figure eights, she said, "I am not going to argue with a student. I will meet their needs where they are."

Nycole's process of assessing and then trying interventions is typical practice. In fact, the Individuals with Disabilities Education Act's (IDEA, 2004) provision of "response to intervention" requires that schools match evidence-based practices to student needs and monitor their progress *before* considering a disability classification. Nycole observed her student's response to her interventions and saw improved focus and attention.

What if these efforts did not work? A next step is to ask for school support. In such a case, a health teacher asked behavior specialist Ash Hall to observe an inattentive student. After talking with other teachers and observing the student at lunch, recess, and in other classes—and using the assessment approaches discussed in Chapter 2—Ash and the health teacher discovered that the problem only occurred in health class. The teacher reported that the student could not focus enough to share when it was his turn, so they made an initial assumption that the student was avoiding talking in front of peers. They devised a simple strategy to try: offering him a cue before his turn to enable him to prepare. It didn't work.

Next, they tracked where the student sat. He was next to the only south-facing window in the classroom, and the afternoon sun beamed into his eyes. His inattention was prompted by the environment; he was sensitive to the light. They not only moved the student but also created accommodations with sensory breaks, provided sunglasses, and offered the student the use of the school sensory room. This student had attention issues in only one class, and he responded well to the interventions. There was no need to consider an evaluation for ADHD.

In the school context, ADHD is not a clinical diagnosis. It is a *classification* under one of the categories listed in IDEA, the federal special education law. Whether or not a student has an ADHD diagnosis outside the school setting, they still need to qualify under IDEA to receive specialized supports in school.

Let's explore what happens in the school context for 3rd grade student Rena, whose attention challenges were chronic and resistant to interventions. Collaborating with the behavior specialist to conduct observations, Rena's teacher found that the student had off-task behaviors at multiple times during the day and in different school settings. Rena got out of her seat and talked to peers frequently in the classroom, in art class, and at lunch. They found that Rena's behaviors were most likely the result of seeking attention from peers and that a root cause could be lack of interest in course content. The behavior specialist worked with teachers to try different strategies, such as increasing peer work in class, but she needed more support. The off-task behaviors interfered with her academic performance, and she was not making progress. The teacher and behavior specialist requested testing for ADHD.

After a discussion with Rena's family, who agreed to the testing, the school psychologist initiated an evaluation for all potential needs. The assessments included background interviews from home and school; rating scales and interviews that focused on behavior, social interactions, attention, and executive functioning at home and with two teachers at school; and previous and updated observations. The school psychologist administered individualized cognitive ability and academic skill tests in reading, writing, math, and communication. After the school psychologist synthesized test results, a team consisting of the family and staff from multiple disciplines (general education, special education, speech therapy, counseling, and school administration) met to review the results and determine a classification.

They first considered whether the evaluation was sufficient to identify all the student's needs—and the answer was yes. The team next looked at whether Rena could be served in general education alone, meaning without the support and services provided by special education professionals. If the answer were no—that she couldn't be served in general education alone—then the team would determine whether she had benefited from appropriate instruction and whether cultural or language factors indicated a special education need. If cultural or language factors were not involved, then the team would consider a disability category best suited to the needs outlined in the evaluation synthesis.

There are 13 disability categories to choose from in IDEA. One of these is "other health impairment" (OHI), which includes ADHD. IDEA defines OHI as individuals "having limited strength, vitality, or alertness, including a heightened alertness to environmental stimuli, that results in limited alertness with respect to the educational environment due to a chronic or acute health problem and adversely affects a child's educational performance" (U.S. Department of Education, 2004). This definition also includes health conditions such as diabetes, epilepsy, and heart problems.

In Rena's case, the team qualified her for special education services under the classification of OHI for ADHD because evaluation results showed that ADHD might best explain her educational performance challenges.

It's important to notice several things about this process. The classification system is IDEA, the federal special education law, and the team's decisions are guided by the law. ADHD does not have its own category, like specific learning disabilities or autism spectrum disorders do. ADHD is part of OHI, a category unique to IDEA that encompasses both physical and mental health conditions.

Further, IDEA has nothing to say about ADHD itself. Instead, the school psychologist has the authority to lead the use of evidence-based practices in the assessment of ADHD to determine classification. The school psychologist may also use information from a different classification system, the one used outside schools: the *Diagnostic and Statistical Manual for Mental Disorders* (DSM). The DSM has the current consensus definition of ADHD and is the first place to go when asking, What is ADHD anyway?

What Is ADHD Anyway?

Now in its fifth edition (American Psychiatric Association, 2013, 2022), the DSM-5-Text Revision (TR) describes ADHD as a mental disorder with three characteristics: a persistent pattern of inattention, hyperactivity and impulsivity, or both. A diagnosis of ADHD with *inattention* requires the presence of at least six (five if age 17 or older) of the nine following symptoms:

1. Often fails to give close attention to details or makes careless mistakes in schoolwork, at work, or with other activities.
2. Often has trouble holding attention on tasks or play activities.
3. Often does not seem to listen when spoken to directly.
4. Often does not follow through on instructions and fails to finish schoolwork, chores, or duties in the workplace (e.g., loses focus, gets sidetracked).
5. Often has trouble organizing tasks and activities.
6. Often avoids, dislikes, or is reluctant to do tasks that require mental effort over a long time (e.g., schoolwork or homework).
7. Often loses things necessary for tasks and activities (e.g., school materials, pencils, books, tools, wallets, keys, paperwork, eyeglasses, mobile telephones).
8. Often is easily distracted.
9. Often is forgetful in daily activities.

Similarly, a diagnosis of ADHD with *impulsivity and hyperactivity* requires the presence of six (five if age 17 or older) of the following nine symptoms:

1. Often fidgets with or taps hands or feet, or squirms in seat.
2. Often leaves seat in situations when remaining seated is expected.
3. Often runs about or climbs in situations where it is not appropriate (adolescents or adults may be limited to feeling restless).
4. Often is unable to play or take part in leisure activities quietly.
5. Often is "on the go," acting as if "driven by a motor."
6. Often talks excessively.
7. Often blurts out an answer before a question has been completed.
8. Often has trouble waiting their turn.
9. Often interrupts or intrudes on others (e.g., butts into conversations or games).

For a combined diagnosis (including both inattention and impulsivity/hyperactivity), clinicians must identify at least six symptoms (five if age 17 or older) from each of the two symptom lists. The final requirement is that those six symptoms (a) have been present for at least six months in a persistent pattern in two or more settings, (b) interfere with daily functioning, and (c) cannot be explained by another DSM diagnosis.

As you can see, the DSM-5-TR description of ADHD is a list of criteria that clinicians use to make a diagnostic decision. You may recognize symptoms related to attention and attention interferences already described in this book. "Is often easily distracted," for example, can refer to both selective attention and the off-topic external interference called distraction.

Let's now take a look at the relationship between the DSM and attention research.

Connections Between the DSM and Attention Research

What would happen if you were transported to the early 1900s to study children's patterns of inattentive or impulsive behaviors? You might see children interrupting one another, saying they forgot what they were supposed to do, or looking for something they misplaced. The behaviors are not new; they are enduring, from the first observations documented in a research journal (Still, 1902) to the DSM-5-TR (2022) description familiar today.

The DSM descriptions, however, are not necessarily based on up-to-date research. Instead, the DSM is created by experts using research knowledge to develop consensus on criteria for the purpose of creating a common language for clinicians. This poses a problem for ADHD research; there isn't necessarily a direct connection between the criteria and the various theories of ADHD—or the research on attention, for that matter.

To solve the research problem, Mueller and colleagues (2017) took advantage of a framework developed by the National Institute of Mental Health (NIMH). They linked the NIMH framework to the DSM ADHD criteria and to results from various research traditions to come up with the seven primary challenges someone with ADHD may experience, called "functional domains." These are as follows:

- Selective attention
- Sustained attention
- Working memory
- Cognitive flexibility
- Response inhibition
- Response precision
- Temporal processing

Right away, you will recognize *selective attention, sustained attention*, and *working memory*. *Cognitive flexibility* (the ability to shift thinking or behaviors in response to the environment) is sometimes related to alternating attention.

The other three functional domains have been studied frequently alongside ADHD. *Response inhibition* (Barkley, 1990, 1994, 1997) refers to the difficulty in stopping—or inhibiting—a behavior or actions that are not required or appropriate. Someone with a response inhibition challenge may interrupt you when you are talking, bring their own mental interferences into the conversation, or succumb to distraction rather than focus on the task at hand. Self-regulation practices typically are used to help individuals inhibit their responses.

Closely related to response inhibition is *response precision*. Response precision is the ability to react to a particular stimulus at the place and time the stimulus occurs (Kofler et al., 2013). Think of the precision handling of a car. To avoid hitting a car moving into your lane unexpectedly, you expect your axle to turn away as soon as you move the steering wheel to avoid an accident. The axle turns at the right time and place, not a millisecond after you expect it. An example of human response precision would be answering a question right after it is asked, instead of remaining silent. Physical activity and yoga (Montalva-Valenzuela et al., 2022) have shown significant results in promoting response precision.

Finally, *temporal processing* refers to the perception of time—the ability to understand how long a task may take or the duration of time just past (Marx et al., 2022). Examples would be underestimating, believing an assignment will take 10 minutes when it actually takes one hour, or overestimating, as when waiting in line feels like "forever" but it's really only been four minutes. Cognitive load reduction strategies can help with temporal processing, such as building in small steps to a task and using a countdown clock during activities (Luman et al., 2008).

Recognizing these functional domains can clarify that a DSM diagnosis, and the criteria used to make it, is part of a larger picture of understanding both ADHD and other attention issues. Let's now look at some misconceptions that can arise from relying on the DSM alone.

Misconceptions About ADHD Diagnoses

As previously noted, the purpose of the DSM is to create a common language for clinicians. A diagnosis provides access to support outside school; in school, school psychologists can refer to the DSM during the IDEA classification decision-making process to provide students with needed resources. The popularity of the DSM, however, has led to misconceptions about ADHD—namely, that the DSM ADHD criteria are established fact or that ADHD has a specific biological cause (Edwards et al., 2014; Erlandsson et al., 2016; Koutsoklenis & Honkasilta, 2023). Understanding the misconceptions will help educators make good decisions about how best to address attention challenges in the classroom. Let's look at these two misconceptions now.

Misconception: ADHD Criteria Are Established Facts

This is not the case. The diagnostic criteria change over time with adjustments in expert consensus, not necessarily in response to scientific advancements (NIMH, 2009).

Although ADHD has a long history dating to the late 1700s (Faraone et al., 2021), English pediatrician George Still is credited for the written descriptions in the 1900s, claiming in 1902 that highly active children had a "moral control defect." This label evolved to become "minimal brain damage" in the 1930s, reflecting the impulsive behaviors observed in survivors of the 1918 influenza pandemic who developed encephalitis (Kahn & Cohen, 1934).

The first DSM appeared in 1952, listing 60 disorders. ADHD made its debut in the second edition (DSM-II) in 1968, one of a new total of 185 disorders. It was called "hyperkinetic reaction of childhood." The DSM-III (1980) label of "attention deficit disorder" shifted the focus from hyperactivity to attention. Finally, the DSM-IV in 1994 identified the three distinct ADHD characteristics as we know them today in the DSM-5-TR: predominantly inattentive, predominantly hyperactive-impulsive, and combined.

Today, ADHD in the DSM meets the "standard criteria... of a mental disorder" (Faraone et al., 2021, p. 793). But researchers disagree on whether inattention or other impairments are central to ADHD and about the criteria themselves (see "Learn More" at the end of this chapter). For example, the age of onset of ADHD, first given as 7 years old (in the DSM-III-TR) and later changed to 12 years old in the DSM-5, is arbitrary (Epstein & Loren, 2013), and the DSM's definition of ADHD itself is circular. As explained by Koutsoklenis and Honkasilta (2023), "if an individual has [ADHD], it is because [they are] inattentive, disorganized, and hyperactive-impulsive, and if an individual is inattentive, disorganized, and hyperactive-impulsive, it is because [they have] ADHD" (p. 3).

As research continues to wrestle with these inconsistencies, it is crucial to understand that a diagnosis of ADHD is a *practical* one: to support those with ADHD symptoms (Wienen et al., 2019). Treating ADHD as a defect of the child is counterproductive. Although medication may alleviate some ADHD symptoms for some students, other nonmedical, research-based strategies have proven effective.

Misconception: ADHD Has a Biological Cause

Research on the origins of ADHD has not identified a biological cause. Gene and brain imaging studies show small and indistinguishable differences between those with an ADHD diagnosis and those without, and these differences also are implicated in other non-ADHD disorders (Dillon & Craven, 2014; Faraone et al., 2021; te Meerman et al., 2017) or simply reflect being younger than classmates (Caye et al., 2020; Sayal et al., 2017). A recent international consensus statement (Faraone et al., 2021) acknowledges that the "genetic and environmental risks [that it reviewed are]... not necessarily specific to ADHD" (p. 794). The recent DSM-5-TR (2022) also summarizes the absence of a biological marker for diagnosis and that a "meta-analysis of all neuroimaging studies do[es] not show differences between individuals with ADHD and control subjects" (p. 73). Challenges also remain regarding disentangling environment from genetics, methodological issues with twin studies, and results not relating to ADHD at all (Cecil & Nigg, 2022; Koutsoklenis & Honkasilta, 2023).

Many associated environmental factors correlate with ADHD diagnoses. These include exposure to toxins (lead, pollutants), certain nutritional deficiencies, and events in utero. Other environmental factors are sexual abuse, physical neglect, low family income, lack of solar intensity, lack of sleep, and death in the family (Faraone et al., 2021; te Meerman et al., 2017). ADHD can also be associated with social crises like a pandemic, intergenerational and racial trauma, hunger, or simply teaching practices that don't reflect how people learn (Beck & Beck-Gernsheim, 2002; Goodwin, 2010; Richards, 2013). A current hypothesis (Sonuga-Barke & Kostryka-Allchorne, 2023) also proposes that "online attentional demands" (p. 974) of consistent screen usage during brain formation could lead to attention problems.

School staff can only work with the best evidence available, and thus far, research on ADHD does not point to precise causes. These students, like all students, have strengths as well as challenges. Focusing on student strengths—asset-based thinking—is a more productive approach for both student and teacher. Research on the strengths of students with ADHD points to creativity, emotional intelligence, and social skills (Climie & Mastoras, 2015; Climie et al., 2019; Hai & Climie, 2022). As teachers get to know students' strengths, along with their inattention patterns and the likely root causes (see Chapter 2), they can support them more effectively in the classroom (Mitchell & Read, 2011).

Teachers sometimes lack confidence in managing behavioral challenges in schools (Walter et al., 2006). When teachers see that they can change behaviors, such as by using the principles in this book to create conditions for attention, they find greater satisfaction in seeking out ways to support positive behavior and are less likely to resort to punishment for obvious off-task behaviors (Mikami et al., 2019).

Understanding these two misconceptions helps counter the belief that medication *must* be used to treat ADHD and is the best, if not only, option for alleviating ADHD symptoms (Gualtieri & Johnson, 2008; Molina et al., 2009).

Medication for ADHD

When you think of ADHD, do you think of medication? Most teachers do (Schatz et al., 2021). It's highly likely that, if a child has a diagnosis or classification of ADHD, they will also have a medication prescription. The most recent statistics on prescriptions dispensed by U.S. pharmacies for ADHD stimulant medications show that from 2014 to 2019, rates increased from 5.6 to 6.1 per 100 individuals (children through adults), ranging from 1.0 to 13.6 per 100 across states (Board et al., 2020). In 2019, the highest prescription rates were for boys between 10 and 19 years old, with one in four receiving prescriptions (one in eight for girls). However, dispensing for children ages 0 to 9 decreased significantly during this period, and dispensing for those ages 10 to 19 stayed about the same or decreased slightly. Despite study limitations, the trends show that stimulant prescriptions are common.

Schools do not have a role in asking families about medication decisions. If a family discloses medication use, they might solicit input from a teacher, such as what time of day the teacher notices increased or decreased attention or impulsivity or if they observe changes in academic performance that could be affected by medication. But keep in mind that cognitive load, limited access to recess, hunger, or other challenges can also interact with behaviors.

Teachers are not responsible for monitoring students' medications. A school nurse may have the duty for dispensing, or there may be accommodations for medications in an individualized education plan, such as having water available for the student. But teachers should have accurate knowledge of what medications are used to treat ADHD. Teachers who observe ADHD symptomatology may be the first to notice changes in attention behaviors that are possibly related to medication, and they can report these changes to families.

When we think of ADHD in medical terms, we might expect that ADHD medications come from a careful analysis of the connection between brain functioning and behavior, leading to the development of a drug that works on those brain mechanisms. But there's no biological test for ADHD that can inform the development of a medication. Instead, researchers tested chemical compounds and observed reactions.

In 1937, a physician discovered that children with problem behaviors became more organized and calmer when given amphetamines (Bradley, 1937). The research team continued testing amphetamines in children for the next 12 years, consistently observing "subdued" behaviors, such as walking instead of running and playing quietly instead of disrupting others. Children who were used as controls also showed similar effects (Bradley, 1950; Bradley & Bowen, 1940; Bradley & Green, 1940). Graduate students of these researchers were the first to refer to methylphenidate (Ritalin) as an amphetamine specifically for children classified as hyperkinetic (Laufer et al., 1957).

In 1961, the United States Food and Drug Administration (FDA) approved Ritalin for children with behavior problems (FDA, 2021). The first rise in stimulant use for children occurred in the 1960s, followed by the first federally funded study on methylphenidate (Mayes & Rafalovich, 2007). In the 1970s and following decades, a hypothesis suggested that ADHD is associated with low activity of the brain chemical dopamine—and that methylphenidate increases dopamine in the brain (Volkow et al., 2001, 2009; Wender et al., 1971).

This history is important to know when we encounter potential misinformation about ADHD medications (e.g., that medication was created specifically to "treat" ADHD). It's equally important to understand the central hypothesis of ADHD as a *dopamine deficit* and that methylphenidate increases dopamine in a brain region called the caudate nucleus, thereby increasing the motivation to perform mental tasks (Westbrook et al., 2020).

Dopamine is known for its role in motivation, in either seeking or avoiding a goal (Wenzel et al., 2015). When we engage in a behavior beneficial to us—like eating a nice meal, hugging people we love, or being curious and learning new information—the chemical rewards us by making us feel good, reinforcing the pleasurable activity. Dopamine also can be *too* rewarding, playing a central role in addictive behaviors, such as continuously scrolling on social media, watching episode after episode on Netflix, playing endless hours of video games or slot machines, and seeking illicit dopaminergic drugs like cocaine.

Dopaminergic stimulants are at the center of controversies regarding methylphenidate and drugs in the same stimulant class (Adderall, Vyvance, Adhansia) used for ADHD. These controversies focus on fears of addiction, overdose, or substance abuse. These fears have been invalidated in the research (e.g., prescribed doses do not get to the brain fast enough), and proponents of stimulant medications for ADHD cite their effects in improving selective and sustained attention and decreasing impulsivity and hyperactivity (Boland et al., 2020).

Stimulants are not associated, however, with long-term improvement or a decrease in symptom severity over time (Riddle et al., 2013; Smith et al., 2010), although some longitudinal studies showed a relationship with lower risks of repeated suicide attempts, sexually transmitted diseases, and teenage pregnancy (Chen et al., 2018; Hua et al., 2021; Huang et al., 2018). Some long-term studies have shown adverse effects of stimulant medications related to high blood pressure, cardiovascular events, slower growth rate, and weight (Díez-Suárez et al., 2017; Powell et al., 2015; Smith et al., 2010; Vitiello et al., 2012), whereas others dispute these effects or their severity (Biederman et al., 2023). Researchers submitted applications to the World Health Organization (WHO) in 2018 and 2020 for inclusion of methylphenidate for ADHD on the WHO Model List for Essential Medicines. Unclear about the evidence for benefits versus harm, the WHO rejected both applications (Ribeiro et al., 2023; Storebø & Gluud, 2021).

The FDA approved the first nonstimulant medication, atomoxetine (Strattera), in 2002. Atomoxetine works primarily on norepinephrine (Garnock-Jones & Keating, 2009), making it neither dopaminergic nor a stimulant. It's considered an alternative to stimulant medications because of fewer side effects and less potential for addiction and for those who do not respond to stimulants. However, norepinephrine works indirectly on dopamine, still affecting the primary chemical thought to be low in people with ADHD.

ADHD medication can be helpful for short-term alleviation of symptoms, but the risks it poses may make some parents avoid it. After a student is diagnosed or classified with ADHD, a parent may share the information with a physician if they want to explore treatment with medication. But what comes next in school?

What Happens After an ADHD Classification?

Students with an ADHD classification through IDEA have an individualized education plan (IEP). It's helpful to know what to expect of such plans and how they relate to supporting students with attention challenges. For example, you may expect to see behavior goals on the IEP for students with an ADHD classification. But in one recent sampling of 183 IEPs for high school students with ADHD, only 51 percent had goals that would guide strategies to help with behavior (Hustus et al., 2020).

Let's take a brief look at the four components of IEPs: present levels of performance, annual learning goals, special education and related services, and accommodations.

Present Levels of Performance

The IEP begins with *present levels of performance,* the results of assessments conducted in the evaluation, including areas in the average range for the child's age and specifics about strengths and needs.

In Rena's case, her performance levels were as follows:

General Intelligence
- Wechsler Intelligence Scale for Children (WISC), fifth edition (Wechsler, 2014): average scores in verbal comprehension and processing speed, high average score in spatial reasoning, below average score in working memory
    - Strengths from these scores: age-appropriate ability to access and apply acquired word knowledge; graphomotor skills, short-term

visual memory, and concentration; strong knowledge of part-whole relationships, attentiveness to visual detail, and visual-motor integration

— Weakness from these scores: needs in attention, concentration, and ability to register, maintain, and manipulate visual and auditory information in conscious awareness

Academic Performance

• Wechsler Individual Achievement Test (WIAT), fourth edition (Wechsler, 2020): scores in the average range for reading, writing, and math, with the exception of a low average score in reading comprehension

— Strengths from these scores: age-appropriate word reading, decoding, and phonemic proficiency, written expression, spelling, math calculation, and problem solving

— Weaknesses from these scores: some difficulties with understanding written language

Social and Emotional Status

• The Behavior Rating Inventory of Executive Functioning (BRIEF), second edition (Gioia et al., 2000): The cognitive regulation index was clinically elevated in all subareas (initiation of activities, working memory, planning, and organizing), with the exception of average monitoring of tasks and organization of materials. The emotional regulation index was clinically elevated in the areas of shift and emotional control. The behavioral regulation index was mildly elevated in behavior inhibition and clinically elevated in self-monitoring.

— Strengths from these scores: skills when starting a task to organize materials for the task and monitor progress toward completion

— Weaknesses from these scores: skills to control and manage cognitive processes and problem solve effectively; regulate emotional responses and adjust to changes in environment, people, plans, or demands; move freely from one situation, activity, or aspect of a problem to another as circumstances demand; emotional control as it relates to fluctuations in mood; skills in regulating behavior through self-monitoring

• Conners, third edition (2008): Both parent and teacher scales showed average scores in hyperactivity/impulsivity, aggression, and peer relationships, but very elevated scores in inattention (T scores of 81 and 76);

learning problems (T scores of 73 and 90); and overall executive functioning (T scores of 71 and 81)

- — Strengths from these scores: skills in not being restless, not moving around a lot, or not being impulsive; control of anger and no issues with defiance; age-appropriate friendships and social connections
- — Weaknesses from these scores: poor concentration and attention, difficulty keeping mind on work, careless mistakes, distractibility; problems with learning or understanding academic material, needs extra explanations; loses things for work and difficulty with getting started on projects

Vision, Hearing, Motor, and Communication
- Showed scores in average ranges

Challenges in these present levels affect Rena's ability to engage in expected academic tasks effectively. She will require assistance for skill acquisition in cognitive and emotional regulation to participate successfully in school and engage in academic programming.

Annual Learning Goals

The goals should match the needs. For example, Rena's problems with working memory and cognitive regulation, combined with a strength in perceptual reasoning, might lead to a goal like this: Rena will follow multiple-step directions provided with visual support 80 percent of the time, as measured by teacher observations on a 1–5 rating scale. For Rena's at-risk area of emotional control, this might be a goal: Rena will identify emotions and use related coping skills 80 percent of the time, as measured by a self-evaluation rating scale.

Notice that both goals are behavioral, indicating actions the student can take that the teacher can observe and document. This is what you are looking for, behaviors like developing a routine, creating a plan, setting priorities, identifying when to use a particular skill, staying on task under certain conditions, or labeling and regulating emotions. The next sections describe where and when the interventions will take place, as well as the explicit instruction the teacher or assigned adult will use to work with Rena to practice and support her independent implementation of strategies when in-the-moment opportunities arise.

Special Education and Related Services

The environment for Rena's goal of following directions likely would be the general education classroom. But the environment for the goals of identifying emotions and using coping strategies could be the regular classroom *and* a related service of counseling outside the classroom for 30 minutes weekly. Both the following directions goal and the coping strategies goal require specific steps and explicit teaching for Rena to move from practice with an adult toward independence.

The intervention for following directions uses chunking to decrease cognitive load and a visual checklist to help with self-regulation. The teacher will break down the directions into steps, provide explicit instruction and repeated practice of the steps, and use a visual checklist for Rena to mark "partially complete," "complete," and "have a question."

The coping intervention may be similar. The teacher might provide explicit instruction on using the mood meter by modeling, then practicing identifying moods in the morning, after lunch, and at the end of the day, and teaching the coping strategies of breathing, meditation, or perspective taking.

Accommodations

Accommodations differ from interventions. Interventions are systematic changes that teachers make to develop or improve student skills, whereas accommodations provide a "differential boost (i.e., more benefit to those with a disability than those without) to mediate the impact of the disability on access to the general education curriculum (i.e., level the playing field)" for students with disabilities (Harrison et al., 2013, p. 556).

Teacher Venessa Kayrell describes accommodations this way: "If my own child cannot reach the shelf that the water glasses are on to get a glass for water because they are thirsty, I have two choices. I can watch them flounder and tell them to climb on the counter and get creative to figure it out, or I can give them a step stool and allow them to get the glass that they would not otherwise be able to access."

An accommodation helps the student reach the goal, as opposed to lowering expectations about their ability to reach it—for example, if Venessa had moved the glass down to the child. The child still needs to be able to get the glass, just as they need to meet curriculum standards in the classroom. Venessa adds a rationale for the accommodation: "It is my responsibility as a loving adult in their life to help them access it. It does not mean to give them the glass of water, if all they need is a step stool."

A typical accommodation on an IEP for students with ADHD is extended time for annual state tests (Lovett & Nelson, 2021). Other accommodations have shown benefits, such as guided notes, technology (timers or text-to-speech), space that limits distractions, changes in the environment to limit distractions, and options for breaks (Konrad et al., 2009). Such accommodations also are available for students not classified as having ADHD under IDEA, but who qualify for accommodations because of an external diagnosis and a need in the school setting under Section 504 of the Rehabilitation Act.

Accommodations may help, but strategies promote more on-task behavior during instruction and independent work. For example, researchers tested the accommodations of support for organization, extended time, and using teacher notes against three interventions of organizational training, self-management, and note-taking instruction (Harrison et al., 2020). Results showed that the interventions were more effective than accommodations in helping students improve their attention to task, organization, and note-taking skills.

✓ Try This: IEP Review

Compare the sections described here with an IEP of one of your students. Scan the document for each section: present levels of performance, annual learning goals, special education and related services, and accommodations. What kind of tests and scores are listed? What are the annual goals and services, and how do they relate to what might occur in your classroom? What accommodations are listed, and how do these differ from the services? Finally, consider strategies in the next section that can align to the student's strengths and needs as noted in the IEP.

ADHD and the Five Principles for Promoting Attention

How much influence can a teacher have on the success of students with ADHD? Lots!

Student success is built on relationships between students and teachers. This is especially true for students with ADHD. A meta-analysis of studies (Ewe, 2019) conducted between 2008 and 2018 found a common theme: teachers feel less emotionally close and have greater conflict with students who have ADHD than with students who don't. As a result, these students feel rejection, have more conduct problems, and ultimately have lower academic achievement.

Teachers who have negative relationships with students will have challenges implementing any of the five principles for promoting attention. As teacher Brittney Lasko (2020) explains,

> I have found myself guilty of viewing my students with ADHD, and their [behavioral] tendencies, as a "deficit," creating frustrated and negative feelings toward them, and wondering why they could not just follow instructions and listen when I requested them to listen. (p. 29)

The good news is that the opposite is also true. When teachers couple patience and a positive attitude with knowledge of how to support students with attention challenges, they can positively influence student attention—and academic outcomes (Sherman et al., 2008).

The five principles for promoting attention are highly relevant for students with ADHD. Here is a brief reminder of the root causes and their associated principles for promoting attention.

- Does not know what to do or how to do it. *Principle for promoting attention: reduce cognitive load.*
- Does not find the task not meaningful, relevant, or interesting. *Principle for promoting attention: incorporate students' background knowledge.*
- Lacks a variety of ways to interact with the content. *Principle for promoting attention: integrate multiple modalities.*
- Does not feel a sense of belonging in the classroom. *Principle for promoting attention: nurture positive relationships.*
- Lacks a sense of autonomy or capacity for self-monitoring. *Principle for promoting attention: teach self-regulation.*

The strategies that follow are from the ADHD literature and focus more on individuals than on groups and more on chronic inattention rather than everyday off-task behavior or mind wandering. Choose those that best fit the needs of your students and classroom.

Attention Principle 1: Reduce Cognitive Load

Speech language therapist Liza Selvarajah works with students who have attention difficulties. In one class, she observed 7-year-old Ava not responding quickly enough. A music teacher came to the class to play the ukulele for the students during music time. When leaving, the teacher said goodbye to each student. When the teacher got to Ava, she said, "Goodbye, Ava!" But Ava just stared at the teacher. The teacher repeated, "Goodbye, goodbye, goodbye!" to Ava, but the girl was "not having it." The teacher finally let it go; after she left the classroom, Ava said, "Bye!"

When getting a blank stare in response to a question, teachers may be inclined to repeat themselves, like the music teacher, or say something like, "I am talking to you" or "I asked you a question." Instead, Liza suggested a new strategy: start saying goodbye on one side of the class semicircle, beginning with Ava so that she is the first to hear it. The teacher says goodbye to Ava first and then moves on to other students, so that by the time the teacher finishes, Ava will have had enough time to be ready to say goodbye.

Cognitive load is the amount or difficulty of information in working memory; when there is too much, students don't understand what to do or how to do it. Ava is not the only one potentially having too much in her working memory. You've probably experienced this yourself, for example, while driving a car, listening to GPS directions and the radio at the same time. You turn down the radio to enable your working memory to focus on your destination without the extra cognitive load coming from the radio. Observing Ava, Liza assumed that she may have had too many stimuli for her working memory, which affected her response precision. The classroom teacher confirmed that Ava frequently had delayed responses.

Now imagine your students with multiple stimuli in their working memory: your spoken directions, peers whispering, materials to organize, thoughts about the past weekend, students around them, or upcoming lunch. They may have difficulty with a functional area of attention, such as being too quick or slow to respond. Or you may need to repeatedly remind students to greet adults entering the room for the students to take notice of them.

Wait time is a strategy for reducing cognitive load. Liza's adaptation—to present the prompt (saying goodbye to Ava first), turning to say goodbye to the other students, and then returning to Ava at the end—gives the student more wait time. Like other strategies we discussed for reducing cognitive load in Chapter 3 (talking less, chunking content, using stepping stones, segmenting time, and reducing interferences), offering wait time can help reduce cognitive load.

Here are some quick-start strategies for individual students with inattention issues.

Use a countdown clock. If a student is off task, offer them a countdown clock. Explain its purpose, which is to let them know how much time they have and help them use that time to start or continue their task. Pull up a device's timer function or purchase a physical countdown clock. Let them know that you'll check with them to see how they think it worked. Some students may turn toward their task and sustain attention, but for others the clock can be a distraction.

Supply a "Get Ready–Do–Done" template (Ward & Jacobson, 2014). The template features three columns for the task, dividing the paper into sections labeled To Get Ready, Do, and Done. Under the heading To Get Ready, a student can list materials, information they need and how they might get it, or even breathing or stretching activities. The task itself is the Do. If the task is small enough, such as completing three math problems, that item may be all that needs to be listed in that space. But if the task has five or more steps—such as reading five paragraphs and writing the takeaway next to each—then a checklist can go in the Do column. Finally, the Done column can include where to submit the task or a reward for having completed it (such as going outside for five minutes).

Ask students what they want to know or do next. At the end of a lesson, a teacher may often ask, "Was anything unclear? Do you have questions?" only to be met with blank stares. Students may be mentally sifting through lots of information, or they may not even know where to begin to answer this question. Remember K-W-L and consider asking, "What is one thing you learned? What do you know now? What do you want to know next? What do you want to do next?" As you experiment with asking these questions, students will start to focus on what they will do next. You may get more insight into what students *did* attend to and how you can help with the immediate next step in their learning.

Researchers call examples like these *high-salient, low-load conditions* (Martinez-Cedillo et al., 2022). They help keep focus and reduce attention interferences. They also help alleviate the pressure students may feel to respond or the confusion or neglect that could occur when they don't. Liza says it may be best to look at it from Ava's perspective: "Honestly, I don't know if I would want to say goodbye if an adult was forcing me to say goodbye to them."

Attention Principle 2: Incorporate Students' Background Knowledge

Imagine one of your students with consistent off-task behaviors. Yes, that one; you always say to yourself that they're not paying attention because they don't like the topic. The fact is, students need connections to their experiences to pay attention. We can learn about students by asking what they do and read at home and with whom they interact, and we can use this information to make useful connections to lessons. For example, each floor in a student's apartment building can be steps in a math problem; their home language shares roots in newly introduced vocabulary words; a historical figure also took care of siblings; and the conflict between two characters in a book is similar to that in a favorite video game. The more we know our students, the better connections we can make in the classroom.

Following are some quick-start strategies to use to create meaningful connections with students who display persistent inattention.

Ask students how they help around the house. Ask students which of their household chores they like best or how they like to help at school. They may like organizing the classroom, cleaning the whiteboard, or being a teacher's helper, which can offer appropriate rewards to students who seek teacher attention. For those who seek peer attention, rewards can include reading to younger students, working with a friend on a project, or teaching a concept to a peer.

Find out what they do with their friends and family. Do they grocery shop? Relate ingredients or costs to mathematics. Do they like riding a bike? Relate the places they go with places on a map, or relate bike riding itself to science concepts like centrifugal force. Do they enjoy playing video games? Ask how characters in a story relate to characters in a game.

Learn about places where they have lived and the languages they speak. If you discover that the student's family immigrated from another country or that the student uses words or phrases in a language other than English, relate new vocabulary to what it might mean in their country or language. You also can compare policies, government structures, and traditions in other countries in social studies or language arts classes. Choose stories to read that reflect students' heritage or family structures.

These are all ways to make meaningful connections to encourage attention. As described in Chapter 3, they require knowing individual students and their successes within school, as well as their cultures, interests, and experiences outside school.

Attention Principle 3: Integrate Multiple Modalities

In one study, teachers were directed to give puzzle instructions to 7-year-olds diagnosed with ADHD in one of three ways: speaking only, gestures only, or gestures coordinated with spoken words. The authors (Wang et al., 2004) provided the following example:

> Teacher speech: "How about the red piece there? What do you think?"
>
> Teacher gestures: Points to the corner of a puzzle piece to give clue to the student (no words).
>
> Teacher speech and gestures: "Try to replace the triangle with the circle. See what happens." At the same time, the teacher points with one hand to the triangular piece, while making a circle with the fingers of the other hand. (p. 6)

Children's average on-task time was 13 seconds with verbal instructions only, 35 seconds with gestures only, and 56 seconds with gestures and words combined. Gestures—either alone or with words—helped the children sustain attention longer, perform better, and have a higher puzzle completion rate (Wang et al., 2004). Gestures introduced the use of multiple modalities.

As we know from Chapter 3, multiple modalities are the various ways we learn. We read, listen, and watch, and we write, draw, speak, move, and touch. Multiple modalities differ from common static, language-focused expectations. Below are some quick-start strategies to offer multiple ways to engage students with persistent inattention.

Practice gestures. Using gestures to give directions—alone or with speech—adds the visual to the verbal for multimodal learning. Teachers frequently use their hands to clarify directions—for example, by saying "We'll discuss [or, "We just discussed"] three main points," holding up one, then two, then three fingers for the concepts. You also can move your entire body, stepping in one place, moving to a second place, and then to a third place in front of the classroom, saying each point as you move. Choose points to emphasize; break apart the content, use pointing or other gestures as you speak to clarify, and observe student attention.

Encourage drawing and creating visuals. Drawing shapes involves motor movement, which research long has related to increased attention (Carson et al., 2001), contradicting beliefs that "paying attention" just means sitting still and concentrating on a single aspect of the environment. Just as gestures along with words are helpful in presenting material and directions, having students create their own graphic organizers, mind maps, and even comics or graphic stories can aid attention.

Make room for movement. It's not surprising that simple physical activity, like the FUNterval activity I described in Chapter 3, helps with the core symptoms of inattention, impulsivity, and hyperactivity, as demonstrated by research on students with ADHD (Seiffer et al., 2021). Movement can refer to moderate to intense activities, such as walking, biking, jumping jacks, skipping, jumping, and running. But it also includes yoga and meditation, which have helped improve attention and behavior for students with ADHD (Jensen & Kenny, 2004; Mehta et al., 2011).

Movement can be useful for the whole class or just one squirmy student. Some students may want to help put away materials, wipe off the board, or gather student papers. Some may benefit from shifting to alternative seating, such as floor cushions, that allows more movement. Middle and high school students may want to change location to work on a new task or sit on a ball or stand while working.

Attention Principle 4: Nurture Positive Relationships

1. "I believe my teacher likes me."
2. "My teacher and I are working toward goals we both agree on."
3. "My teacher and I agree on the things I need to do to help me improve my schoolwork."

Would you want a student with ADHD to endorse all three of these statements? If so, you would favor a *working alliance*, in which there is a bond between you and the student (Statement 1); you and your student have agreements on goals (Statement 2); and you and your student agree on tasks (Statement 3). The statements are from the Classroom Working Alliance Inventory (Toste et al., 2015, p. 35), which has shown that ratings of high collaboration with teachers predict greater academic competence and school satisfaction for students with classifications like ADHD, compared with their peers (Toste et al., 2014).

We know that teachers tend to have fewer positive relationships with students they view as having attention problems (Ewe, 2019). Students see it, too. Compared to students without ADHD, students with ADHD report less care and support from teachers, more negative relationships, more controlling classrooms, and feelings of incompetence (Rogers et al., 2015; Rogers & Tannock, 2013). Recognizing this possible pitfall, teachers may need a targeted approach that promotes a positive bond and leads to collaboration.

Here are some ways to create this working alliance.

Create a close bond. The interview questions we listed in Chapter 3—asking students about family activities, the video games they play, and social media preferences—can help form a bond. Others target student aspirations, such as, What is something that makes you happy? What is your biggest dream in life? Questions can also be school-related, such as, What is one thing you have done in school that makes you feel accomplished? What is one thing you would want to change about school? Bonds begin to form as the teacher follows up on the questions, incorporates answers into the work, acknowledges the student, and continues positive conversations with the student throughout the year.

Make agreements about goals. Do your students know the goal of a task? For example, Nycole rearranged the classroom space so that one of her students could run to the carpet during transition time. Her conversation with the student might have sounded like this:

> Teacher: During your transition to the carpet, what is your goal?
>
> Student: To get to the carpet.
>
> Teacher: Yes, but I will add on to that. The goal is to sit on the carpet safely. What do you think about that goal?
>
> Student: OK, safely.
>
> Teacher: Can we agree on that goal with a fist bump?

The objective here is to have a conversation with the student about the goal and come to an agreement, confirming it with a handshake or fist bump, or writing it down on paper.

This same strategy works in middle and high school. Select an obvious behavior (swearing, leaving seat) that you want your student to replace with a more appropriate behavior (take a breath, communicate with the teacher) that doesn't interfere with their peers' learning. Discuss the goal ("What's a good replacement for swearing?") and then agree on it together ("Can we agree to focus on this goal for one week?"). When a student is hesitant, work on refining the goal and agreement ("What would be a better goal?" "What's a better goal to agree on?").

Make agreements about tasks. Tasks are steps to a goal. For Nycole's student, she might say, "To get to the carpet safely, your task is to look up before you start, run in this section, and look before the home base slide." They might practice the task together to ensure that the student agrees with the task. For an academic goal, such as completing five math problems, the teacher and student might discuss the steps to get there: complete one problem and check with a peer or teacher; have a method for communicating to the teacher that you're stuck, such as by placing a yellow card on the desk or using a signal known only to the teacher; set a time to complete the problems.

The focus here is to develop a purposeful relationship with a student who has persistent off-task behavior to help overcome the tendency among teachers to have negative relationships with students with ADHD (Ewe, 2019). Students with ADHD who report a close bond with their teachers also have increased academic motivation (Rogers et al., 2015).

Students with ADHD are aware they may have different routines than other students. They may have an interventionist who comes into the classroom to support them; they may leave to see another adult; or they may have accommodations, such as extra time or a separate space for taking tests. Noticing these accommodations, students will sometimes make negative judgments about their peers with ADHD (Mueller et al., 2012).

The stronger your working alliance with students, the more you'll notice when a stigma might be playing out. For example, if you notice that a student appears uncomfortable taking a test in a different place than other students or looks around at their peers to see who notices when an adult comes into the room to work with them, ask them how they're doing. Provide other options for where to take the test or for when or how they might work with the other adult. If needed, you can work together to create an alternative positive environment for the student within the parameters of the service or accommodation on the IEP.

Positive relationships also rely on family communication; the more support students get outside school, the lower the risk for continued ADHD symptoms (Duh-Leong et al., 2020). Share with the student's caretakers your working alliance with the student and any effective supports you use. These might include a countdown clock or wait time (for cognitive load); connections to student interests (for incorporating background knowledge); visuals combined with verbal communication (for multiple modalities); or any of the self-regulation approaches that follow.

Attention Principle 5: Teach Self-Regulation

You may recall Danny Vương teaching his students about the mood meter at the beginning of the year, with its four quadrants showing low and high energy and pleasant or unpleasant feelings. Recognizing feelings and when they occur is the first step to self-regulation. You can experiment with this yourself. Say you hear some sad news (unpleasant, low energy) or feel anxious about work (unpleasant, high energy), but you need to teach right now. What do you do? It's likely you'll recognize the feeling and maybe use a breathing strategy or quickly write down the interfering anxious thoughts. Finally, you turn toward teaching the lesson.

It's not always easy for adults, let alone for children and adolescents whose brains aren't fully developed, to make the switch from recognizing feelings to attending to a task. This can be even more challenging for students with functional impairments related to ADHD. Actively teaching self-regulation strategies is both necessary and beneficial.

Self-regulation is the act of consciously behaving to inhibit one's response to attention interferences (Barkley, 1997). Self-regulation enables a person to maintain attention in working memory, select and alternate attention to the current task, and develop the self-control to plan and monitor decisions—all activities related to the functional difficulties of ADHD (Mueller et al., 2017). The following strategies encourage self-regulation for students with persistent off-task behaviors and ADHD functional impairments.

Teach emotional recognition. The mood meter offers a concrete way to recognize feelings. There are others. If you're an elementary teacher, you may have a poster or some other display of faces or emojis that shows and labels feelings. Research has shown that strategies for regulating emotions are especially helpful in early adolescence (Murray et al., 2022), particularly for those with attention challenges whose emotional regulation needs continue into adulthood (Christiansen et al., 2019).

If a student yells at you or another student, a negative feeling is behind that behavior. After a yelling incident, some teachers will look at a feelings chart or an emoji poster with their student to identify the feeling together. If it's anger, the teacher and student can discuss what happened before the anger or the feelings that anger masks, such as sadness, embarrassment, shame, guilt, stress, or worry.

Your next step can be asking the student if they would be open to sharing the feeling with you instead of yelling, writing down the frustrating thought and sharing it with you, or asking you what to do if the yelling occurs again. You then can make an agreement to collaborate on the behavior change. The goal is for a student to notice and label how they're feeling, identify triggers for those feelings—and stop and think before responding.

Teach perspective taking. Sometimes a teacher might see a young student take a toy away from another. One common thing to say to the offending student is "Tell them you're sorry." The child may apologize—because you told them to—or they may refuse. Instead, take the student aside for a conversation that acknowledges what happened. You might ask questions such as these: "How do you think the other student felt when you took the toy? What might help them feel better? That can also help you two have a good relationship. What do you think?"

This isn't only for younger students; young adults can benefit from conversations that respect their perspective, like asking specifically about how *they* view the situation, then asking questions like, "Would you mind experimenting with me by jumping into their shoes?" "What do you think they were thinking or feeling?" "Tell me how that's similar to your perspective." "Tell me how it's different from your perspective." End with asking for a suggestion for a resolution or providing two options for the student to consider. Explicitly teaching perspective taking is especially helpful for students with attention challenges (Marton et al., 2009).

Coach students to self-talk. A student getting started on a task may find it helpful to repeat the directions aloud. Let's say a student gets distracted on the way to the pencil sharpener; they might repeat, "Sharpen pencil" to help keep themselves on track. And when you give directions, ask, "What do you understand about the directions?" This encourages students to repeat the directions, which lets you know what they understood. Or have them repeat task instructions back to you by saying, "Tell me what you're going to do first." Then use their language or gestures to move on to the next step. This enables students to hear their own language related to keeping on task (Barry & Haraway, 2005; Parker et al., 2011). Eventually, they may remind themselves, either silently or overtly, of the task goal or their place in the process to direct them back on task.

Teach organizational skills. Organizational skills are related to time, space, and tasks. Students with attention challenges have difficulties keeping school materials organized to maintain focus and minimize distraction and tracking their completion of the task (Evans et al., 2014, 2018). Teaching these skills has been shown to improve academic performance and even family relations (Abikoff et al., 2013; Bikic et al., 2017).

For **organizing time**, use a planner, either on paper or on the student's mobile phone, listing classes, assignments, and due dates, with phone reminder notifications before due dates. Teachers should check not only what is written in the planner, but also its accuracy (Abikoff & Gallagher, 2009). Students can also use a daily calendar with hours blocked out for meetings, classes, and activities.

For **organizing space,** students may have their own organizational strategies, such as putting materials for class on the top left of their desk, if they are right-handed, so that they can write on the bottom right side. Or they might put documents in a physical or virtual folder and writing utensils in a certain place in their backpack. For **organizing tasks**, students can use checklists or mind maps of project tasks, lists of items to accomplish, or steps in an assignment.

Interventions with self-regulation components that are one-on-one and personalized have a substantial effect on students with ADHD (Moore et al., 2018), especially for on-task behavior (Reid et al., 2005). Although spending additional time practicing self-regulation strategies with a student may initially seem difficult, it pays dividends over the school year for the student and the entire class.

Conclusion

Author Paulo Freire was a child of the Great Depression, living in Portugal, hungry and in poverty. This experience taught him that hunger and the challenges of an impoverished background were what interfered with learning—not insufficient interest or an inability to learn. As a high school teacher, Freire discovered that children in poverty had difficulty learning because of their environments—and because their schooling was trying to fit them into a rigid system, rather than enabling them to learn and expand their lives. This insight led him to affirm the individual development and transformation of students and become an eloquent advocate for incorporating students' backgrounds and social contexts into their education.

For students with persistent attention challenges, an environment like that experienced by both Paulo Freire and Gillian Lynne (at the beginning of this chapter) is not conducive to learning. If we persist in trying to force our students into a one-size-fits-all system, particularly students with ADHD, then we will persist in getting frustrated at their off-task behaviors. Instead, if we get to know students, connect who they are with what they learn, offer goals that are both ambitious and attainable, support their ways of learning, and teach self-regulation skills, then we can create an environment that nurtures attention and student success. Students with attention challenges, or an ADHD classification especially, need teachers who understand what ADHD is and how to support them in their learning and success.

Chapter Reflection: Pick a Strategy

Reflect on the five principles of attention related to ADHD—reduce cognitive load, incorporate students' background knowledge, integrate multiple modalities, nurture positive relationships, and teach self-regulation. Recall what you do now and what you would like to try. Consider a student who may need more help with attention than others. Then,

1. Choose a new strategy or one that builds on a previously used strategy.
2. Plan specific content you would like to try the strategy with.
3. Write down your steps to incorporate the strategy.
4. After you try it, make any needed modifications, then try using it with other students or content, or revise the questions or steps.

Learn More: Perspectives of ADHD

The approach to the ADHD discussion in this chapter is practical: students displaying consistent inattention that interferes with their progress need supports, and an ADHD classification is a way to get help. ADHD is one of the most controversial psychiatric diagnoses, and this chapter's approach is based on multiple perspectives in the study of ADHD to provide knowledge of its history, identification, and controversies to promote informed decisions about creating conditions for attention. Several notable controversies focus on what ADHD is and the classification system.

A prevailing theory is that ADHD is an inability to self-regulate behavior (Barkley, 1997). Barkley (2022) contends that this behavior is *emotional impulsiveness*, which has been central to the history of ADHD from prior to George Still's work, and therefore should be a core, rather than associated ADHD feature, in the DSM. Researchers have criticized this theory for failing to include *attention* as central to the description of ADHD (Bush, 2010); offering no explanation of how behavioral inhibition and attention interact (Luo et al., 2019); suggesting that ADHD may better be considered an attention regulation deficit (Hinshaw, 2018); and positing emotional impulsiveness may be an ADHD subtype accounting for heterogeneity (Sonuga-Barke et al., 2023).

Critiques of the DSM criteria themselves include a failing to take account of people with the same diagnosis but lacking overlapping criteria (NIMH, 2009) and the diagnostic reliability of the variation in symptoms (e.g., mild, moderate, severe) across clinicians (Epstein & Loren, 2013). Notably, ADHD research has shown that ADHD symptoms are unstable over time and heterogeneous among individuals, suggesting a need for a continuum in the diagnostic criteria as opposed to the DSM's single category (Nigg et al., 2020). This symptom variation and heterogeneity are among the rationales used in recent descriptions of ADHD as "neurodiversity," meaning that individuals with ADHD symptoms are mismatched with their environment (Sonuga-Barke & Thapar, 2021), much like Sir Ken Robinson's depiction of Gillian Lynne at the beginning of this chapter.

All of these are places to start in your ongoing learning about ADHD. Further reading may include the article by Mueller and colleagues (2017) discussed at length in this chapter linking ADHD to attention research and the brain, which can help with how to spot attention-related problems. Another is the editorial by Sonuga-Barke and Kostyrka-Allchorne (2023) that explores the practical aspects of these top concepts.

5

Creating Conditions for Attention

In this chapter, teachers tell their own stories from their classrooms about creating conditions for productive attention. They use varied strategies, drawing on their backgrounds and teaching experience. You have met some of these teachers throughout the book; now you will see their rhythms and routines for creating conditions for student attention.

These teachers stand out not only for their expertise in finding ways to create conditions for attention, but also for their understanding of student needs. As students, they had their own experiences of feeling invisible or misunderstood and encountering teacher biases about their own attention.

Each also identifies as a teacher of color. The U.S. education system was built around the narrow experiences of the white people who colonized the land; eliminated those who land it was; enslaved individuals who built the economy; and created legal exclusions of immigrants seeking solace, rejecting their descendants. In every aspect of education, white voices and perspectives are taught and heard.

Our implicit biases, ingrained from this long history, persist, and so inequitable treatment continues. Now, Black, Indigenous, and other students of color are the majority in U.S. schools. It is crucial to elevate and center diverse voices to understand the experiences of those who can be unsupported and judged when it comes to issues of attention.

In Chapter 1, we discussed attention as an *effect*, not a cause. Doing so enables us to shift from treating inattention as an individual fault to understanding students' reasons for being off task or inattentive, with the goal of creating a better learning environment. This is an intentional paradigm shift, establishing a new mindset. It's about students controlling their own learning, as opposed to teacher control that's aimed at obedience. In this new mindset, teachers continually make the most of cognitive load management, student interests, multiple modalities, relationships, and self-regulation to improve students' understanding.

If Today Is a Hard Day for You...
Seon Kim, California

When Seon Kim was a teaching assistant in a 2nd grade classroom, she worked with a teacher whose notion of "paying attention" was having students sit up straight with their hands folded and their feet on ground while tracking the speaker. There would be negative consequences for students who leaned back in their seats, pushed their seats backward, or leaned forward with their hands on the desk.

This reminded Seon of when she was a 2nd grade student herself. She once got in trouble for talking to a student next to her, and the teacher sat her on the floor to work by herself as a punishment. "It completely traumatized me," she said. "I didn't speak in class after that. I didn't want that to happen to anyone else."

One day, Seon asked the teacher if she could take a student, who was in trouble yet again for being inattentive, for a quick walk. She thought the walk would help the student work off some energy. "They were just being kids, and I didn't want them to get in trouble," she said. To her surprise, the teacher agreed. Seon soon began to use these quick walks for that student and others who frequently showed "inattentive" behaviors. Sometimes Seon would race them, running quickly back to the classroom. It always seemed that the run improved things; the students enjoyed the physical movement, and it helped them focus afterward.

After getting a job as a 7th grade teacher, Seon knew that she didn't want to punish students. But she also found that she couldn't give everyone her personal attention, especially because her focus was mostly on those with disruptive behaviors. As she explained, "When I first started teacher training, I was taught to write on the board—and still somehow face the class. I thought, 'I don't know how to do that. The students cause a scene every time I turn my back.'"

Under the principal's direction, she tried to manage the class's attention by giving demerits and three warnings before sending students to the school dean. But this wasn't helping the situation, and she felt the approach didn't fit her teaching style. "I was tense at the end of the day," she said. "I was becoming the type of teacher I didn't like." It didn't make sense to Seon that teenagers with developing hormones and growing minds would have to focus all day—or get punished.

Seon needed a different approach. Initially, she used little attention tricks while showing math problems on the board in front of the class, like skipping a step as she talked through a math problem. Students perked up to point out the mistake, and if students didn't notice what happened, then they asked their peers. She then started scribbling over her writing to cross out what she wrote and turning letters into characters, like flowers and garden gnomes. The same thing happened: students started talking about her drawings and making suggestions about what to draw next.

Her intentional mistakes and drawings drew student attention to the activity. It was a great start, but it didn't always last or help focus students on the actual math. Seon remembered that she had doodled in school as a student and that doodling had helped her pay attention in class. She gave all her students sticky notes. "Do what you want with these notes," she instructed. "Just always be appropriate. You can doodle. You can write questions to me. You can write math rules on them."

Seon noticed increased attention with the sticky note strategy. She watched students doodle while listening, doodle to refocus a wandering mind, make a flip book, write questions and math notes, and stick the notes on their desks. She saw what she thought was self-regulation; students who would normally say "I don't know," instead referred to the sticky notes for answers. She also watched students physically refocus. For example, they would reposition themselves, lean forward, do a quick stretch, then focus on a sticky note. They were moving their bodies to come back to the task, and it seemed they understood that it was OK to daydream and that they didn't need to be embarrassed if their minds wandered at times.

The sticky notes were working great for whole-class attention. Some students, however, still had difficulty staying on task. The only way to improve student attention across the board, she thought, was to get to know students individually. In this classroom, like other classrooms, students often had traumas or struggles related to their home environment. At the beginning of the school day, Seon stood at the door when students walked in, asking them for a factoid or a positive anecdote. The anecdotes provided information and a quick "temperature check" of how students were feeling.

Seon wasn't able to ask probing questions to figure out what was bothering some of the students. Students would say things like, "I don't want to talk about it... there's nothing wrong." Students feared being embarrassed, like one student whose family was about to be evicted. Another student lived with a large family in a one-bedroom apartment; sharing the classroom with peers who had new mobile phones or new Air Jordan sneakers was difficult for him. As Seon noted, "When students come in consecutive days looking tired, and they don't want to talk about it, trying to grab their attention doesn't work."

So she added a new purpose to the sticky note routine. She said, "If today is a hard day for you, just jot your name on the sticky note, and put the note on my desk. This will signal to me that today is not a day to call on you, and I won't ask you what's going on unless you'd like to talk."

Later on, Seon started teaching middle school at a new school. Veteran teachers warned her about a student. "She triggers easily," they said. Seon knew she needed to introduce the sticky note strategy to the class the first week and thought it might help. She explained to the students that they could doodle on the sticky notes or jot down notes on them. Or they could put a note on her desk to let her know they were wrestling with an issue and that she shouldn't call on them that day.

A few weeks into the school year, Seon saw a sticky note from the student she had been warned about on her desk. She thought, "Oh, no." She watched the student carefully that day. The girl had been playing with the other students, but now she had her nose in a book. She wasn't paying attention to anything else.

"I left her alone," Seon said. "Every now and then, I'd say 'Hey, could you give me 10 minutes of the lesson, then you can get back to your book?'" The student agreed, paying attention to the lesson for 10 minutes and then returning to her book. They kept this exchange going for a while.

After a few days passed, Seon saw another sticky note on her desk from the same student; the girl's notes started coming every few weeks. On most days, the student was a voracious reader, and if Seon asked her to put down her book, she would do it. However, on the days she put the sticky note on Seon's desk, she'd become aggressive if asked to stop reading. But once they started with the 10 minutes on and then back to the book, this ritual became "their thing," and the student started to pay more attention in class.

As Seon observed, "The name-on-the-desk idea helped build trust and safety. Once this student said, 'I saw my dad yesterday.' This was more than she had said to any other teacher. One small thing, and it helped the relationship and increased her attention to task."

Seon never thought that one strategy—sticky notes—would increase attention. Some students used the notes for taking notes or marking pages, which helped them break down their assignments or self-regulate on tasks. But those who used them for emotional regulation were memorable. They felt seen and heard, and as a result, they were willing to shift their attention back on task.

My Teachers Didn't See Me

Sandra Golden, Ohio

When Sandra Golden was in 5th grade, her family moved from a high-poverty community, where most of her peers were Black like her, to a working-class community, where most of the students were white. That was when she started to feel invisible at school.

This was the 1970s in the Cleveland area where, during Sandra's 5th through 12th grade years, race riots occurred in the community. There was anger and discord around her, but she always paid attention in school, although she wasn't talkative or active like other students. The more vocal students were presumed to be engaged learners, and they received the teachers' attention. Students who didn't pay attention also had the teachers' eyes on them. Teachers would raise their voice at those students, isolate them in the corner or hallway, or send them to the principal's office. Sandra was relieved she wasn't targeted like that, but she felt that no one noticed her or encouraged her. She felt invisible.

As an adult, Sandra began teaching Adult Basic Literacy programs. The classes were a mix of high school–age students, working and unemployed adults, and business owners. She paid close attention to the quiet students and found ways to engage them in learning. She capitalized on student strengths, such as encouraging students to produce creative works or asking various students to help her manage the classroom.

But Sandra also saw many students behaving like her nonattentive peers when she was young. They talked to other students, looked around the room, and ignored the teacher's directions. She did not want to raise her voice at the off-task students like the teachers she remembered, so she started listening to students' responses to her redirections. They asked questions like, "Why do I have to be here?" "Why do I have to read?" "Why do I have to read this book?" "Why do I have to write?" She realized that the inattentive students did not find school meaningful or relevant.

She had a breakthrough in a summer program teaching middle schoolers reading and writing. The topic was historical figures, and Sandra announced that Martin Luther King Jr. would be the first person they would study. She saw the students' reactions. They immediately turned away from her and started to talk with one another. One student spoke up. "No," the student said. "We have been learning about MLK since kindergarten!"

Other students agreed, but Sandra was up to the challenge. "How about, with your wealth of knowledge, you lead our class discussion on MLK?" she said. She had the student who confronted her and another student lead the discussion. She organized students into groups, provided a timeline and ways to prepare, and worked with the students throughout the process. What the students presented was not traditional, like MLK's famous speeches. Instead, they dug into his family background, looked at other people he knew, and clarified the civil rights context. "They took it to a different level," she said. That experience showed Sandra that her goal wasn't to "teach," but rather to create structures for attention and to coach and advise.

That was when she shifted her classrooms from being teacher-centered to student-centered. She let go of her control. She likened her approach to that suggested by educators who wrote about student-centered classrooms, like Gloria Ladson-Billing's (1997) culturally relevant pedagogy and Parker Palmer's (1997, 2017) *The Courage to Teach*. "Teaching is for your students," she summarized. "You have to do it in a way that they can do it without you."

Years later, during the first full year of the COVID-19 pandemic, Sandra was the director of academic excellence at an elementary community school for grades K–4. There were not enough teachers when students returned from virtual to in-person learning during the second half of the school year, and she found herself in an unlikely position: teaching kindergartners and 1st graders.

Sandra used a variety of instructional methods and strategies, based on the students' academic levels. Some did not yet recognize letters of the alphabet, the sounds of consonants, sight words, or word patterns. She used familiar techniques that she had used with older students: she modeled her own thoughts and encouraged students to share what they knew. But when she asked students to walk up to the front of the room to point to letters on the wall and share, many students just looked around or down at the ground.

In her previous classes, her students had been part of creating rules and structures, so with these 60 students, she decided to create literacy centers with about four students in each, all with hands-on or paper-and-pencil puzzles for learning letters, letter-sound awareness, letter patterns, and common words.

It took students three weeks to follow the directions and routines that led to effective learning. The first week focused on rules. Students discussed expectations, such as being kind to friends and materials, working cooperatively, and raising hands for teacher attention, and then they practiced in the groups. During the second week, Sandra increased the time in the literacy centers by having the students work in groups for a short period, then rotate to a new center. She provided new guidelines for moving: "Walk and move with your group. Listen for when I call your table, such as 'Table 3, stand up.'"

By the third week, the classroom felt like a community. Students wrote, drew, discussed, and created stories connected to their letters and words. Sandra observed and facilitated. The students had different interests and skills, so those with sustained attention in an activity were allowed to stay at a center longer. When students appeared distracted or disinterested, they would move to other centers or work on individual activities, such as drawing, coloring, or writing. Teacher-focused small groups also were adapted for other students. The centers enabled Sandra to watch and listen to individual students so that she could maximize on-task behaviors in ways that met their needs.

Sandra never forgot her experience of feeling invisible in school. The first day of her multi-age classes, she noticed three students toward the back of the class. She positioned herself near them to get to know them, understanding that being quiet did not mean they were not interested. "Teachers didn't see me," Sandra says today. "I now know I am an introvert. And I want the quiet or shy students to feel seen." Now, as a teacher, she sees the whole class—the quiet ones who may be on task or even off task with their minds wandering, as well as those with obvious off-task behaviors—so that she can make learning meaningful for all students.

 ## Building Confident Students

Adrienne Hayes, Colorado

Adrienne Hayes remembers her 3rd grade teacher's words: "You're not going to get very far if you act like that." What Adrienne was "acting like" was "zoning out" when the teacher gave directions, as many a 9-year-old would do. This had a big effect on her then; she thought the teacher knew all about her, her future, and where she could—or couldn't—go. "It was quite painful," she recalls. That experience set the stage for Adrienne. If she didn't know what to do because her mind had wandered as the teacher was giving directions, she felt she couldn't ask for help, so she just faked her way through.

That 3rd grade experience did not end in 3rd grade. In Adrienne's senior year, her English teacher's idea of a model student was one who sat quietly, raised their hand, and asked questions. She started skipping class to go to the band room to practice, a place where she felt the teacher was supportive of her learning. As a result, the English teacher called her parents to threaten that she might not graduate. The intervention returned her to English class, but Adrienne still didn't feel included.

As a 4th grade teacher now, Adrienne knows that attention varies. She doesn't explain directions only one time. She shows the information visually, repeats the directions in a different way, or has students check with one another on the directions before starting the task. This way, students know their teacher cares enough about them to be sure they have the information.

Caring goes beyond initial directions for a task, however. Adrienne creates a class structure for her 32 4th graders that enables them to build on their background knowledge, engage in multimodal learning, and self-regulate through projects where she can support their attention along the way.

One six-week action research project focuses on animals. During the first week, Adrienne models a K-W-L (Know, Want to Know, Learned) process (Ogle, 1986) on an animal. The next two weeks are collaborative, and students jointly choose an animal. Usually they choose bears, because, being from Colorado, they know there are bears in the mountains. They launch into learning about bears using research and writing skills, including how to find credible texts, select information, and generate questions. Together, they list what they know and generate questions for what they want to learn in the K-W-L chart.

Over the final three weeks of the six-week unit, each student selects their own animal for the K-W-L process. Adrienne creates a checklist to help them self-monitor their progress. When they go off task, she can ask what checklist step they are on to determine what caused their inattention so that she can help. For example, if they do not understand the step in the "K" of the process, she might ask them to think about one interesting fact or what surprised them the most about their animal to then add to that step.

Adrienne knows when a student hasn't been paying attention because they lag behind the other students or haven't asked questions or sought help. She pulls some of those students into a separate group and says, "Tell me what is tricky about this part." Usually students need clarification on the directions, and after getting that information, they then go over the exemplar she provides. Some will say, "OK, I got it—I'm ready to go!" and return to their group to work. Others might need different support, such as help with reading skills. This process helps Adrienne differentiate for inattention; some inattention is the result of a student needing help with a step, and some requires more specialized support.

This support could not happen without Adrienne's focus on building relationships. Conversations at the beginning of the year start with what it means to be a student: a student takes risks, a student feels brave and confident, and a student in the classroom community helps others. Students answer the question, When someone is struggling, what does it mean to "help" them, rather than tell them what to do? Adrienne also sets the expectation that she's looking for *learning*, not just students having the right answers. The students can learn from all types of answers, and Adrienne wants to see what they are learning from the process.

The conversation about what a community means to them is ongoing. Adrienne often provides examples like, "Class, pause for a moment. I know that you are in your thinking, but I want to highlight Ashriya. She is checking in with a neighbor next door because she was unsure what to do. Ashriya, tell us about that." Students like to point out when they did the same thing as Ashriya. Once students grasp the concept, habits start forming, and they start using learning language with one another, such as, "I can see how you thought that. I thought that, too!" Then they share their new thinking. This means that the community is growing and that students feel safe.

Today, Adrienne is firm: her idea of a model student is one who is collaborative. "We seldom make advances in isolation," she says. This partnership in dialogue, exploration, and discovery drives students' attention, and, ultimately, learning.

It's About Connecting to Students' Interests

Sean Miller, Virginia

"I was what teachers would call an inattentive student," observes high school teacher Sean Miller. He doodled and drew caricatures and other images throughout his schooling. It wasn't until a 12th grade presentation on college that he really felt noticed. He was in the back of the room drawing, unmotivated about school, as a panel of speakers talked about college. One of the speakers came up to him at the end.

"I've been watching you draw this whole time," the speaker said. Sean didn't look up, assuming he was about to hear yet another adult criticize him for inattentiveness. But the speaker surprised him: "Have you thought about the art program at the university?"

Sean looked up and asked, "What program?" The moment was life-changing for him. For the first time, Sean felt seen. He applied to the program and was accepted.

Now that he teaches 9th through 12th grade, he sees many students doodling; they seem to be in their own world, disconnected from the space around them. Sean can listen as he draws, but not everyone can do that, so he seeks the right time to approach those students privately and ask what they are drawing. His focus is on building relationships with the students and finding ways to integrate their interests into the class, without judging them for inattention.

Sean has implemented several strategies to foster attention in his classes over the years. Students created comic strips in his U.S. Government class to show what they already knew about the concept of direct democracy in government. They enjoyed selecting the images and planning the frames and the steps in the stories. They also needed support from Sean in a few areas. For students who struggled with images and dialogue, he offered ways to search for or create simple images. For those who struggled with critical thinking and analysis, he slightly reduced the writing requirement so that they could master the concept. And still other students who were highly analytical created a more extensive comic that captured multiple points about the concepts. The results displayed a range of student knowledge, with the comics featuring single to multiple concepts and presenting the material in straightforward and serious, as well as in comical and humorous, ways.

When school went virtual during the pandemic, the comic creation activity helped Sean get to know student interests, their self-regulation capacity, and their conceptual understanding. He could not always tell who was paying attention online or who needed help focusing on the lesson because not all students showed their faces or spoke in the virtual classroom. But when students searched for and selected images, Sean *did* see their interests. Some pulled characters from a cartoon they liked, some selected the first images they found in a search, and some created their own stick figures with the pencil tool. Once he saw their first steps and the list of images they planned to use, he could leverage their interest—or lack of interest—to ask about their image creation and help them over barriers they might have with a concept.

In the 2021–2022 school year, Sean began teaching the first-ever African American history course in his district. An African American himself, Sean was aware of the absence of his own history in the curriculum, despite the central role that African Americans had played in building the U.S. economy while enslaved and excluded, withstanding violence and rising with resilience.

He was excited about teaching those missing perspectives in a comprehensive history course to a new generation. The course was elective. Sean assumed that the students who chose to take it did so from a wish to see themselves in what they were learning or from an interest in finding out what they hadn't learned in general U.S. history courses.

Sean also knew that these students, as interested as they might be, wouldn't always pay attention. He already planned to give them a choice among different modalities to use for their capstone project. The students could create comics, as in his previous courses, or do presentations that involved writing an analysis or using videos or music. For the latter, he brought in music equipment set up for recordings. As he presented these options to the class, he watched their reactions.

In the back row, two students sat looking at each other. At Sean's suggestion of using music for the capstone project, one elbowed the other, giving him a meaningful look. Sean knew he could capture their attention if he found out what their exchange signified.

As class ended, Sean asked the student who had been elbowed whether he'd like to include music in his culminating class project. As a result, the student stopped by Sean's classroom after school and shared song lyrics he had created in response to the Black Lives Matter protests across the United States in 2020. Sean told the student that he had a solid foundation for a capstone project and that he wanted to see how the student would incorporate in that project ongoing course themes, such as human agency. Sean offered a guiding question: How are you going to take what you learn this year and produce new music for your capstone?

This process that began with the student seemingly not paying attention and that ended with the student reflecting on how he could use course content to build on his interests happened in just three weeks. It took multimodal options and a focus on relationship building. Sean noticed that others took note of his interest in that student, which opened up the opportunity to get other students hooked as well. Sean began to focus on talking to students in class and in the hallway between classes.

The end-of-year projects varied from website creation and slideshows to short films. One website focused on colorism, with slides discussing, among other topics, Black hair in the context of history; another website presented material on death rates among African Americans. The short films discussed gentrification, identity, and Black joy. Students included narration, interviews, and poetry in their multimodal productions.

Sean says it is his responsibility to figure out the ways his students learn, then help them understand those ways themselves to maximize on-task behavior and therefore their attention. He brings in what he learned as a student—both from the teachers who judged him negatively and from those who encouraged him—to connect intentionally with individual students and create whole-class conditions for attention.

 ## What to Do When You Flip Your Lid

Danny Vương, Washington State

When Danny was in 5th grade, his teacher was leading the class through making corrections on a paper they had all worked on, when someone knocked at the door. A student sitting next to him stood up, walked to the door, and opened it to let the person in. When the student returned, Danny shared his paper so that his classmate could copy the corrected items the student had missed in the interval. Just then, the teacher walked up to them, took both papers, and ripped them up in front of the entire class.

Danny decided to confront the teacher after the lesson, telling him that he had simply shared the corrections with the student that they had completed together as a class. The teacher responded by taping the papers back together and returning them.

This was the first time Danny advocated for himself. As an Asian American, he was raised to "do what you are told and that the adult was always right." Now, as a teacher, he tells students about one of the rules of Love and Logic as described by Fay and Funk (1995): if you feel that something is unfair, whisper to me, "I am not sure that is fair." Then they talk. Teaching self-advocacy gives students agency—and starts them on the road of self-regulating for attention.

To Danny, the core of self-regulation is to recognize emotions and communicate needs without causing harm to others in the process. He teaches the peace corner and mood meter at the start of the year. Another successful strategy is the **flipped lid** approach (Siegel & Bryson, 2011). Danny uses his open palm and closed fist to model the parts of the brain. With his palm facing students, he moves his thumb to the palm, explaining that the thumb represents the mid-brain structures, like the amygdala, which processes emotions such as fear, and the hippocampus, which relates to memory. Then Danny closes his palm over the thumb (i.e., over the mid-brain) to show a fist. "This is your thinking brain," he explains, "when you are calm." Finally, he opens his hand back up, palm facing the students: "This is when your feeling brain is exposed;

you are emotional, and you cannot think clearly. It is called 'flipping your lid.' When you recognize your lid is flipped, you need to take a breath, walk away, and regulate yourself again."

Danny related a story of a student who used the flipped lid strategy while playing basketball during recess. The player was upset because other players kept calling a foul on him for traveling, but others were doing the same thing and were not called out for it. As the student was getting ready to explode in anger, he suddenly showed the flipped lid signal—palm open, fingers up—and said he needed a moment. Then he walked away from the situation to breathe and self-regulate. Afterward, he and Danny debriefed so that the student could communicate his feelings and let the other players know his perspective. The players ended up making amends with one another and agreed to have someone be a referee the next time they played.

Teaching self-regulation requires modeling. Danny models tools, too, such as the Behavior Reflection template from former 5th grade teacher Laura Candler, owner of Teaching Resources (see www.lauracandler.com). At the beginning of the year, Danny felt he needed to apologize for something, apologized, and then shared how he went about this with the class. He showed students how to use the Behavior Reflection template, which has places for describing the situation, giving your reasons for acting as you did, listing the consequences of that behavior, and providing your plan for improvement.

Let's look at how Danny filled out the template:

1. Description of my behavior: I was late to the "Going Green" assembly.
2. The reasons for my behavior were:
   - I thought it was Wednesday, not Tuesday.
   - I didn't check my email this morning to see the reminder.
   - I was in yellow (on the mood meter) and was too excited to teach writing.

3. The consequences of my behavior were:
   - How do I feel? Guilty.
   - How has my behavior affected others? I made grades 3–5 wait, as well as the actors.
   - Other consequences: My students were rushed during writing (a sudden transition, which they handled well).

4. Plan for improvement: I will write a note to [names] and apologize for keeping everyone waiting. I'll hold myself accountable by talking to my team about this.

Danny reflected on his behavior in front of his colleagues; he also had his colleagues and an administrator sign his apology note to show he follows through and is accountable. He explained to students that everyone makes mistakes, including adults, and that we all need to take steps to repair the harm done.

As the school year continued, students formed the habit of self-reflection, which helped them more frequently alternate their attention from their emotions to the tasks at hand. Regulating emotions with strategies is not punitive, like an isolated time-out; in time-out, students are forced to regulate *without* reflecting, allowing the emotions to continue. Rather, Danny's frame for his class is changing the language from punishment to restoration, enabling students to learn about the causes and effects of behavior. "It's like dropping a cup of liquid," Danny explains. "The *logical* consequence is cleaning it up. *Punitive* is being forced to stay in for recess. When the class offers plenty of self-regulation opportunities, expectations are high, students are accountable, and attention improves."

Being Brave and Safe

Barb Miller, Nebraska

Barb Miller welcomes her 6th grade English language arts class back from lunch: "Give me a thumbs-up if you remember what I said this morning about taking educational risks." All thumbs go up. She has their attention and continues: "I want you to think for 15 seconds to get an answer in mind. When I say 'Go,' turn to your table partner and discuss one truth about learning according to Ms. Miller."

Students are quiet for a few seconds, and then, on cue, they begin to share their ideas with their partners. Barb has immediately enabled her students to shift their attention from lunch to the topic at hand.

Barb watches their discussions start to fade and speaks slowly: "Finish your discussion in [she counts] 3...2...1... time! Now, as a group, finish this sentence: You will not take educational risks in an environment where you don't feel...." Students exclaim, "safe!"

Barb has spent years getting to this point in setting up positive relationships in which students' voices are heard and students listen and share with one another. These efforts included not only practice but also developing supports for marginalized students within the existing gifted program. She had taught gifted students for her entire career, and she knew that students of color were significantly underrepresented in advanced programs (Patrick et al., 2020). The International Baccalaureate (IB) program in the most diverse high school in Barb's school district reflected the research. Although a majority of students in the school were students of color, only a small percentage were enrolled in the IB program.

As a middle school teacher and a teacher of color, she recalled her own experiences, wishing that her teachers would have had higher academic expectations of her. These students had the same need, and she knew she had to step up and prepare them for inclusion in IB.

Barb partnered with a supportive principal, and together they reviewed and brought the data to administrators. They investigated how students were selected and how they were either ignored or missed. They then created a comprehensive plan to identify, invite, and elevate students. Seven years in the making, a small group of students has become an honors cadre in grades 6–8.

Barb now facilitates a weekly meeting where the honor cadre students learn how to learn, self-advocate, and collaborate. Just like in her English language arts class, her students know that to take educational risks, they need to feel safe. A safe space, she notes, is where students feel brave enough to speak their thoughts. "Why would a brave space be important to me?" she asks the students. "Think about it for a minute, and be prepared with an answer."

One of the students immediately speaks up: "We need to be brave enough to talk about our feelings!" Barb redirects: "I am giving you a minute to think about a response. I am not turning down your answer, Lin—it's good. I just want everyone to think from a clear slate. Come up with your own 'why' and we will share in a minute."

Students are quiet for a minute, then Barb has them share with their table partner. As students are chatting, Barb monitors their discussions and places numbered sticky notes in front of three student pairs.

Barb brings them back: "I heard some great discussion, and you came up with solid responses. I would like to hear from sticky note number 1. What did your pair come up with?"

Carlos responds: "We talked about how it takes bravery to try new things, and you told us to find our passion, so we need to not just do what is comfortable." Barb comments on the power of bravery in discomfort.

But Amira is doubtful. "Ms. Miller," she says. "I have to be honest. I feel nervous about all of this." Barb responds, "Amira, that's fair. This is the second week of school in this new experience. I feel nervous, too. This is a space where we can openly own our feelings and work through them together. It won't happen overnight, but we will continue to build each other up. That's what we do!"

Barb listens as others respond affirmatively to Amira's concern, then she asks everyone to talk about the characteristics of a safe, shared space. Two students take notes on the board. The students suggest that members of a safe space

- Are helpful.
- Communicate with one another.
- Are fun.
- Listen.
- Rely on one another.
- Trust one another.

Barb provides feedback on the list; lets students know they will pick up on the safe, shared space characteristics next time they meet; and thanks them for a productive period.

Barb explains that her fast pace leaves little time for disruption of attention. She uses short chunks of both topics and time to help decrease cognitive load. Within this pacing, students are always doing something multimodal—for example, a choral reading or partner discussion. She facilitates the process, asking such questions as, What makes you say that? How do you know? These questions help students connect to their background knowledge and experiences. When she gets clues that students are not paying attention—for example, when they're not sharing their thoughts or asking questions—she asks, "Where did I lose you?"

In the beginning of her teaching career, Barb created classroom rules herself. But she quickly learned that students are off task and act out because the rules can seem arbitrary to them—like being obliged to stay in their seat for an entire class period or have papers returned, marked in red. Barb now starts with *bravery* as a concept central to a safe, shared space.

For example, a punitive response to not submitting an assignment does not help with assignment submission. Instead, Barb offers support. She asks questions, such as, What got in the way of getting the assignment done? Do you need additional time? What can I do to support you? Are you learning what you need to learn? She revisits their classroom community rules. If students have missed something, such as homework, they "own" it.

Once students agree to the rules they helped create, they are responsible to one another for following them. Barb models the expected behaviors, such as when someone is left out. She'll ask students, "Are you ready to be a learner today, to hold our sacred space? What needs to happen to get there?"

"Everyone has bad days," Barb says. There are times when students are not ready to be attentive. She tries to catch their attention before it shifts away from the topic at hand. Barb concludes that belongingness is central to attention—and to belong, "bravery and safety are key."

Conclusion

Good teachers intentionally create conditions for attention in multiple ways. They use strategies to reduce cognitive load, incorporate background knowledge, support multiple learning modalities, teach self-regulation—and they know and have positive relationships with their students. One strategy doesn't work for all students and teachers. But these stories from teachers should shine a light on how teachers pay attention to how students pay attention, and how you might, too.

Chapter Reflection: From Then to Now

The teachers in this chapter describe their attention experiences from when they were students themselves, as well as their reactions as teachers. As you recall, when Seon was in 2nd grade, she got in trouble for talking to a student, and the teacher sat her on the floor to work by herself as a punishment. When Adrienne was in 3rd grade and "zoned out," her teacher told her, "You're not going to get very far if you act like that."

We tend to remember these times; take a moment to recall your own. Write it down. Then change your perspective to that of the teacher. If you were the teacher viewing you, what would you do differently? Next, try to think of a student to whom you had a negative reaction. What would you do differently now?

Seon, Sandra, Adrienne, Sean, Danny, and Barb are good at creating conditions for attention, but they can also teach us another important lesson, which is to look to our past to reflect on something that negatively affected us, then turn it into a strength to help others. Career counselor Mark Savickas (2019; Savickas et al., 2005) calls this work "active mastering of passive suffering." When we recall passively feeling invisible or misunderstood—which translated into our own reasons for being inattentive to the task—we can actively master seeing and understanding these issues for our students.

What do you see yourself as mastering now, based on your past experiences in school and with attention?

6

Taking Action for Attention

This book has been a journey to explore an important classroom issue: how you, as a teacher, can create conditions to encourage and support student attention in school.

We took a deep dive into the issues of attention and inattention. We examined the various types of attention (Chapter 1), how to assess for attention and find root causes (Chapter 2), how to promote attention (Chapter 3), and ADHD (Chapter 4). We learned that attention is a complex issue, and we scrutinized our own assumptions about and reactions to student inattention. And you heard from real teachers about their efforts to improve student attention (Chapter 5).

It's a lot!

But keep in mind that teachers every day are using the procedures and strategies outlined here. As with learning any new skill, it may seem hard at first. But if you practice, reflect, and practice again, these techniques will become a seamless part of your classroom routine. The rewards—for both you and your students—will be substantial.

Here are some final thoughts to consider as you continue this important journey.

Turn Judgment into Curiosity

Have you found yourself judging students when they don't pay attention? You may think, "This kid is immature," or "This kid is so ADHD," or "This student just doesn't care about school." Such thoughts are common among teachers struggling to figure out how to capture a student's attention. Now, having read this book, you'll recognize that such attitudes are not helpful to your efforts. Judgments can be a dead end if we're trying to help students, whereas *curiosity* offers a path to understanding and constructive strategies for improving attention.

If you don't judge, great! You were ready to assess attention before reading this book.

But if you do find yourself judging students in these ways, be prepared to confront those judgments and turn them into questions. Think back to the student behavior that led to those judgments. Was it consistent off-task behavior? At what point did you make that judgment?

Consider, instead, how you might assess the student's inattention. When did it occur? What might be the reason for the behavior? What would you do differently if you knew the underlying cause of the behavior?

This book offers a comprehensive process for turning judgment into curiosity and, in turn, into strategies for dealing constructively with inattention issues, for both individual students and the class as a whole. Hold on to that curiosity as you move forward.

You can use this as a reference book on attention. There's always more to learn, more techniques to try, more research offering useful insights. The book offers many reflective questions throughout that you may want to revisit from time to time, as well as a variety of resources for your further exploration.

Assume Students *Can* Pay Attention

A 2015 Microsoft publication titled *Attention Spans* claimed that the human attention span was diminishing from increased exposure to technology, shifting from 12 seconds in 2000 to 8 seconds in 2013, a second less than "the average attention span of a goldfish."

Do you believe this claim? I don't.

Consider the attention spans of people you see around you: adults walking and looking at their mobile phones, children involved in creative play, and teenagers engaged in intense discussions with friends. Those attention spans certainly are longer than mere seconds, so it's not surprising that the Microsoft claim has no evidence to support it (Bradbury, 2016; Subramanian, 2018).

In other consumer-based research on attention spans, Prezi (2018) teamed up with a research group to understand how content and how it is presented resonate across demographics, finding that most full-time employees across generations improved their focus on content over time and became more selective about the content they chose. They also reported difficulties with attention because of multitasking, which we know from this book is alternating attention, which involves three mental operations of disengaging one of our senses (e.g., sight) from one activity or stimulus, moving to another stimulus, and then engaging with this new object.

The diminishing attention span myth persists, however, mainly based on anecdotal observations of alternating attention. It may also persist because excessive screen time can have negative effects on mental health, sleep, and even attention (Domingues-Montanari, 2017; Lissak, 2018; Santos et al., 2022). But it's best to assume that students *can* pay attention, and indeed *want* to pay attention, but may struggle with various interferences. They can learn to monitor their own attention to keep out interferences, such as distractions from devices or excessive device use, but they may need to learn the skills of self-regulation. You can help by explicitly teaching the strategies described in Chapters 3 and 4, which address those issues.

Consider Your Own Attention

If you've thought about your own attention capabilities throughout this book, congratulations! This was intentional. We do this through critical reflection, by becoming aware of and questioning our own experiences and behaviors.

You've seen that, even as adults, we still have attention challenges, although our brains are more developed than those of our students. When we think about our own attention, we engage in self-regulation, monitoring our thoughts, feelings, and behaviors. Understanding our own attention offers insight into our students and helps us teach self-regulation skills, enabling students to see their own patterns of attention and inattention and discover ways to improve.

As you consider your own attention, here are some questions to keep in mind:

- What happens when I turn my attention to a new focus? Where is the selective, alternating, and sustained attention?
- What are reasons for my own off-task behavior? What could be a root cause of my own off-task behavior or inattention?
- How do I get back on track? What conditions or strategies for attention help most?
- How does self-regulation help?
- When I find myself not paying attention, how do I react? Do I feel compassion for myself? Do I ask myself why?

Experiment with Attention Strategies

Don't tackle everything at once. This book contains many principles, processes, and strategies related to attention, as well as an array of reflective questions. The easiest way to approach these and build your confidence in using them is taking them in—in bite-size chunks.

Experiment by focusing on one principle for the whole class—such as "reduce cognitive load"—or focus on just one or two students for whom you think that principle will have the greatest effect. Phase in the strategies, discuss successes and failures with colleagues, reflect on your experience, and adjust as needed.

Experimentation needs data and an evidence-based solution to try. Look at the data in Chapter 2, and try the strategies in Chapter 3 that the data lead you to. Then keep observing and interviewing. Soon, the right strategies will stick, and you'll be ready to try new ones. Through this experimentation, you'll establish a productive cycle of learning for individual students, the classroom, and yourself. Assess, try, test, and adjust. As you try out new strategies, keep in mind the spiral process.

Figure 6.1 summarizes the ideas from previous chapters. It shows likely root causes, principles for monitoring attention, and broad and more targeted strategies to implement. As you move forward, keep these in mind—root causes, principles, and strategies—because they all connect.

Keep in mind that experiments don't always produce answers the first time. Think in terms of continuous improvement and action research methods. Like experimentation, these are structured procedures that include data, assessment, implementation, reflection, and adjustments.

Expand Your Knowledge About Attention

Before starting this book, you may have equated attention with focus, like a spotlight or camera that's either on or off. But we've seen that attention is more complex than just focusing, and it's not an on/off switch because there's not just one type, but multiple ones—selective, alternating, and sustained.

This book gives you the basics of attention, based on cognitive psychology. Research on attention continues in many fields, with studies of the brain holding particular promise for our greater understanding (Posner et al., 2016). Now that you have the basics, you're equipped to create conditions conducive to attention in your classroom. You're also equipped to expand your knowledge of attention, attention research, and its implications for your students. The resources here can help you continue your explorations.

FIGURE 6.1

An Overview of Root Causes, Principles, and Related Strategies

Likely Root Cause of Inattention (Chapter 2)	Principle for Promoting Attention (Chapter 3)	Strategies for Attention (Chapter 3)	More Individualized Strategies for Attention (Chapter 4)
Student does not know what to do or how to do it.	Reduce cognitive load.	• Talk less. • Chunk content and time. • Create stepping stones. • Lessen external interferences.	• Use a countdown clock. • Supply a "Get Ready–Do–Done" template. • Ask students what they want to know or do next.
Student does not find the task meaningful, relevant, or interesting.	Incorporate students' background knowledge.	• Interview students. • Plan lessons with student experiences in mind. • Connect the new with the known. • Build curiosity.	• Ask students how they help around the house. • Find out what they do with their friends and family. • Learn about places where they have lived and the languages they speak.
Student lacks a variety of ways to interact with the content.	Integrate multiple modalities.	• Use varied texts. • Add visual organizers. • Incorporate peer learning. • Introduce intentional movement.	• Practice gestures. • Encourage drawing and creating visuals. • Make room for movement.
Student does not feel a sense of belonging in the classroom.	Nurture positive relationships.	• Say student names often. • Share decision making. • Improve relationships throughout the year. • Set up communication frames.	• Create a close bond. • Make agreements about goals. • Make agreements about tasks.
Student lacks a sense of autonomy or capacity for self-monitoring.	Teach self-regulation.	• Show how to recognize behaviors, feelings, and thoughts. • Set up self-regulation strategies when the year begins. • Use checklists consistently. • Give task-specific feedback.	• Teach emotional regulation. • Teach perspective taking. • Coach students to self-talk. • Teach organizational skills.

Conclusion

Not paying attention is not a deficit of behavior or character. As adults, we learn to monitor and direct our own attention—but we certainly don't do this consistently. We continue to learn about our own cognitive processes and use that knowledge to regulate our behavior.

Human brains are not fully developed until age 25. Our role as educators is to find the best ways to support our students in their process of brain development. You now have the tools and understanding to address the crucial issue of attention in your classroom. So, jump in and get started!

Chapter Reflection: Sharing with Others

You now have a reference book about attention. You're experimenting with assessment and conditions for attention. Are you noticing differences in yourself? In your students? In managing your classroom or teaching specific content? Share your experiences.

Although attention is not an easy concept to explore, you can now link research-based approaches to practice. Choose areas you found intriguing or surprising; see if your colleagues are interested in talking about attention or trying out the strategies themselves. Share your successes and failures; you can all learn from these. Discuss your observations and new understandings with students. And be sure to let parents and families know about your classroom success with attention so that they can help support it.

References

Abikoff, H., & Gallagher, R. (2009). *The children's organizational skills scales: Technical manual.* Multihealth Systems.

Abikoff, H., Gallagher, R., Wells, K. C., Murray, D. W., Huang, L., Lu, F., & Petkova, E. (2013). Remediating organizational functioning in children with ADHD: Immediate and long-term effects from a randomized controlled trial. *Journal of Consulting and Clinical Psychology, 81*(1), 113–128.

Albers, P., & Harste, J. C. (2007). The arts, new literacies, and multimodality. *English Education, 40*(1), 6–20.

Aldahash, R., & Altalhab, S. (2020). The effect of graphic novels on EFL learners' reading comprehension. *International Journal of Applied Linguistics and English Literature, 9*(5), 19–26.

Allday, R. A., & Pakurar, K. (2007). Effects of teacher greetings on student on-task behavior. *Journal of Applied Behavior Analysis, 40*(2), 317–320.

Allen, J. (2008). *More tools for teaching content literacy.* Stenhouse.

American Psychiatric Association. (1968). *Diagnostic and statistical manual for mental disorders* (2nd ed.).

American Psychiatric Association. (1980). *Diagnostic and statistical manual of mental disorders.* (3rd ed.).

American Psychiatric Association. (1994). *Diagnostic and statistical manual of mental disorders.* (4th ed.).

American Psychiatric Association. (2013). *Diagnostic and statistical manual of mental disorders* (5th ed.).

American Psychiatric Association. (2022). *Diagnostic and statistical manual of mental disorders* (5th ed., Text Revision).

Ariga, A., & Lleras, A. (2011). Brief and rare mental "breaks" keep you focused: Deactivation and reactivation of task goals preempt vigilance decrements. *Cognition, 118*(3), 439–443.

Arnold, L. E., Hodgkins, P., Kahle, J., Madhoo, M., & Kewley, G. (2020). Long-term outcomes of ADHD: Academic achievement and performance. *Journal of Attention Disorders, 24*(1), 73–85.

Aronson, E. (1978). *The jigsaw classroom.* Sage.

Ashinoff, B. K., & Abu-Akel, A. (2021). Hyperfocus: The forgotten frontier of attention. *Psychological Research, 85*(1), 1–19.

Atkinson, R. C., & Shiffrin, R. M. (1968, January). Human memory: A proposed system and its control processes. In K. W. Spence & J. T. Spence (Eds.), *The psychology of learning and motivation: Advances in research and theory,* (Vol. 2) (pp. 89–195). Academic Press.

Ausubel, D. P. (1968). *Educational psychology: A cognitive view.* Holt, Rinehart, & Winston.

Awh, E., Belopolsky, A. V., & Theeuwes, J. (2012, July 16). Top-down versus bottom-up attentional control: A failed theoretical dichotomy. *Trends in Cognitive Sciences, 16*(8), 437–443.

Ayano, G., Demelash, S., Gizachew, Y., Tsegay, L., & Alati, R. (2023). The global prevalence of attention deficit hyperactivity disorder in children and adolescents: An umbrella review of meta-analyses. *Journal of Affective Disorders, 339*, 860–866.

Ayres, P. (2006). Impact of reducing intrinsic cognitive load on learning in a mathematical domain. *Applied Cognitive Psychology: The Official Journal of the Society for Applied Research in Memory and Cognition, 20*(3), 287–298.

Babad, E. (1993). Teachers' differential behavior. *Educational Psychology Review, 5*, 347–376.

Baddeley A. (1992). Working memory. *Science, 255*, 556–559.

Baddeley, A. D., & Hitch, G. J. (1974). Working memory. In G. H. Bower (Ed.), *The psychology of learning and motivation: Advances in research and theory* (Vol. 8) (pp. 47–89). Academic Press.

Barkley, R. A. (1990). *Attention deficit hyperactivity disorder: A handbook for diagnosis and treatment.* Guilford.

Barkley, R. A. (1994). Impaired delayed responding: A unified theory of attention deficit hyperactivity disorder. In D. K. Routh (Ed.), *Disruptive behavior disorders: Essays in honor of Herbert Quay* (pp. 11–57). Plenum.

Barkley, R. A. (1997). Behavioral inhibition, sustained attention, and executive functions: Constructing a unifying theory of ADHD. *Psychological Bulletin, 121*(1), 65–94.

Barkley, R. A. (2022). High time preference is a key cognitive deficit in ADHD: Impact on daily life, impairments, and life expectancy. *The ADHD Report, 30*(7), 1–5.

Barry, L. M., & Haraway, D. L. (2005). Self-management and ADHD: A literature review. *The Behavior Analyst Today, 6*(1), 48–64.

Beck, U., & Beck-Gernsheim, E. (2002). *Individualization: Institutionalized individualism and its political consequences.* Sage.

Beghetto, R. A. (2007). Prospective teachers' beliefs about students' goal orientations: A carry-over effect of prior schooling experiences? *Social Psychology of Education, 10*(2), 171–191.

Bennett, B., & Rolheiser, C. (2001). *Beyond Monet: The artful science of instructional integration.* Bookation.

Betts, J., McKay, J., Maruff, P., & Anderson, V. (2006). The development of sustained attention in children: The effect of age and task load. *Child Neuropsychology, 12*(3), 205–221.

Biederman, J., DiSalvo, M., Green, A., Vater, C. H., Driscoll, H., & Faraone, S. V. (2023). Growth trajectories in stimulant-treated children ages 6 to 12: An electronic medical record analysis. *Journal of Developmental & Behavioral Pediatrics, 44*(2), e80–e87.

Bikic, A., Reichow, B., McCauley, S. A., Ibrahim, K., & Sukhodolsky, D. G. (2017). Meta-analysis of organizational skills interventions for children and adolescents with attention-deficit/hyperactivity disorder. *Clinical Psychology Review, 52*, 108–123.

Blachowicz, C. L. (1986). Making connections: Alternatives to the vocabulary notebook. *Journal of Reading, 29*(7), 643–649.

Board, A. R., Guy, G., Jones, C. M., & Hoots, B. (2020). Trends in stimulant dispensing by age, sex, state of residence, and prescriber specialty: United States, 2014–2019. *Drug and Alcohol Dependence, 217*, 108297.

Bobo, L. D., Charles, C. Z., Krysan, M., & Simmons, A. (2012). The real record on racial attitudes. In P. V. Marsden (Ed.), *Social trends in American life: Findings from the General Social Survey since 1972* (pp. 38–83). Princeton University Press.

Boland, H., DiSalvo, M., Fried, R., Woodworth, K. Y., Wilens, T., Faraone, S. V., & Biederman, J. (2020, April). A literature review and meta-analysis on the effects of ADHD medications on functional outcomes. *Journal of Psychiatric Research, 123*, 21–30.

Bradbury, N. A. (2016). Attention span during lectures: 8 seconds, 10 minutes, or more? *Advances in Physiology Education, 40*, 509–513.

Bradley, C. (1937). The behavior of children receiving Benzedrine. *American Journal of Psychiatry, 94*(3), 577–585.

Bradley, C. (1950, January). Benzedrine® and Dexedrine® in the treatment of children's behavior disorders. *Pediatrics, 5*(1), 24–37.

Bradley, C., & Bowen, M. (1940). School performance of children receiving amphetamine (Benzedrine) sulphate. *American Journal of Orthopsychiatry, 10*(4), 782–788.

Bradley, C., & Green, E. (1940, September). Psychometric performance of children receiving amphetamine (Benzedrine) sulfate. *American Journal of Psychiatry, 97*(2), 388–394.

Bradley, M. M., Sabatinelli, D., Lang, P. J., Fitzsimmons, J. R., King, W., & Desai, P. (2003). Activation of the visual cortex in motivated attention. *Behavioral Neuroscience, 117*(2), 369–380.

Broadbent, D. E. (1958). *Perception and communication.* Pergamon.

Brookfield, S. (1995). Adult learning: An overview. *International Encyclopedia of Education, 10*(3), 375–380.

Brookfield, S. D. (2017). *Becoming a critically reflective teacher* (2nd ed.). Wiley.

Brotherson, D., & Santana, L. (2017). *Curiosity and learning: Teach students to ask better questions.* Paper presented at the Learning Forward Annual Conference, Orlando, FL.

Bruner, J. S. (1966). *Toward a theory of instruction.* Belkapp.

Bruni, T. P., Drevon, D., Hixon, M., Wyse, R., Corcoran, S., & Fursa, S. (2017, April). The effect of functional behavior assessment on school-based interventions: A meta-analysis of single-case research [Special issue]. *Psychology in the Schools, 54*(4), 351–369.

Bush, G. (2010). Attention-deficit/hyperactivity disorder and attention networks. *Neuropsychopharmacology: Official publication of the American College of Neuropsychopharmacology, 35*(1), 278–300.

Butler, C. T., & Rothstein, A. (1988). *On conflict and consensus: A handbook on formal consensus decisionmaking.* Food Not Bombs.

Butler, D. L., & Winne, P. H. (1995). Feedback and self-regulated learning: A theoretical synthesis. *Review of Educational Research, 65*(3), 245–281.

Card, A. J. (2017). The problem with "5 whys." *BMJ Quality & Safety, 26*(8), 671–677.

Carlson, K. A., & Shu, S. B. (2007). The rule of three: How the third event signals the emergence of a streak. *Organizational Behavior and Human Decision Processes, 104*(1), 113–121.

Carson, S., Shih, M., & Langer, E. (2001). Sit still and pay attention? *Journal of Adult Development, 8,* 183–188.

Caye, A., Petresco, S., de Barros, A. J. D., Bressan, R. A., Gadelha, A., Goncalves, H., Manfro, A. G., Matijasevich, A., Menezes, A. M. B., Miguel, E. C., Munhoz, T. N., Pan, P. M., Salum, G. A., Santos, I. A., Kieling, C., & Rohde, L. A. (2020). Relative age and attention-deficit/hyperactivity disorder: Data from three epidemiological cohorts and a meta-analysis. *Journal of the American Academy of Child & Adolescent Psychiatry, 59*(8), 990–997.

Cecil, C. A., & Nigg, J. T. (2022). Epigenetics and ADHD: Reflections on current knowledge, research priorities and translational potential. *Molecular Diagnosis & Therapy, 26*(6), 581–606.

Chen, M. H., Hsu, J. W., Huang, K. L., Bai, Y. M., Ko, N. Y., Su, T. P., … & Chen, T. J. (2018). Sexually transmitted infection among adolescents and young adults with attention-deficit/hyperactivity disorder: A nationwide longitudinal study. *Journal of the American Academy of Child & Adolescent Psychiatry, 57*(1), 48–53.

Choi, H. H., Van Merriënboer, J. J., & Paas, F. (2014). Effects of the physical environment on cognitive load and learning: Towards a new model of cognitive load. *Educational Psychology Review, 26*(2), 225–244.

Christiansen, H., Hirsch, O., Albrecht, B., & Chavanon, M. L. (2019). Attention-deficit/hyperactivity disorder (ADHD) and emotion regulation over the life span. *Current Psychiatry Reports, 21*(3), 1–11.

Chun, M. M., Golomb, J. D., & Turk-Browne, N. B. (2011). A taxonomy of external and internal attention. *Annual Review of Psychology, 62,* 73–101.

Clarke, T., Ayres, P., & Sweller, J. (2005). The impact of sequencing and prior knowledge on learning mathematics through spreadsheet applications. *Educational Technology Research and Development, 53*(3), 15–24.

Climie, E. A., & Mastoras, S. M. (2015). ADHD in schools: Adopting a strengths-based perspective. *Canadian Psychology, 56*(3), 295.

Climie, E. A., Saklofske, D. H., Mastoras, S. M., & Schwean, V. L. (2019). Trait and ability emotional intelligence in children with ADHD. *Journal of Attention Disorders, 23*(13), 1667–1674.

Coiro, J., Knobel, M., Lankshear, C., & Leu, D. J. (Eds.). (2008). *Handbook of research on new literacies.* Routledge.

Commodari, E. (2013). Preschool teacher attachment and attention skills. *SpringerPlus, 2,* 673.

Conners, C. K. (2008). *Conners* (3rd ed.). Multi-Health Systems.

Cook, M. P. (2017). Now I "see": The impact of graphic novels on reading comprehension in high school English classrooms. *Literacy Research and Instruction, 56*(1), 21–53.

Cortés Pascual, A., Moyano Muñoz, N., & Quilez Robres, A. (2019). The relationship between executive functions and academic performance in primary education: Review and meta-analysis. *Frontiers in Psychology, 10,* 1582.

Crescentini, C., Capurso, V., Furlan, S., & Fabbro, F. (2016). Mindfulness-oriented meditation for primary school children: Effects on attention and psychological well-being. *Frontiers in Psychology, 7*, 805, 1–12.

Crozier, W. R. (1998). The psychology of embarrassment. *Cognition & Emotion, 12*(5), 715–721.

Csikszentmihalyi, M. (1979). The flow experience. In D. Goleman & R. J. Davidson (Eds.), *Consciousness: Brain, states of awareness and mysticism* (pp. 63–67). Harper & Row.

Csikszentmihalyi, M. (2013). *Flow: The psychology of happiness*. Random House.

Danielsen, A. G., Wiium, N., Wilhelmsen, B. U., & Wold, B. (2010). Perceived support provided by teachers and classmates and students' self-reported academic initiative. *Journal of School Psychology, 48*, 247–267.

Danielson, M. L., Claussen, A. H., Bitsko, R. H., Katz, S. M., Newsome, K., Blumberg, S. J., Kogan, M. D., & Ghandour, R. (2024). ADHD prevalence among U.S. children and adolescents in 2022: Diagnosis, severity, co-occurring disorders, and treatment. *Journal of Clinical Child & Adolescent Psychology*, 1–18.

Darling-Hammond, L., Flook, L., Cook-Harvey, C., Barron, B., & Osher, D. (2020). Implications for educational practice of the science of learning and development. *Applied Developmental Science, 24*(2), 97–140.

DeWall, C. N., Maner, J. K., & Rouby, D. A. (2009). Social exclusion and early-stage interpersonal perception: Selective attention to signs of acceptance. *Journal of Personality and Social Psychology, 96*(4), 729–741.

Dewey, J. (1933). *How we think: A restatement of the relation of reflective thinking to the educative process*. D.C. Heath.

Díez-Suárez, A., Vallejo-Valdivielso, M., Marín-Méndez, J. J., de Castro-Manglano, P., & Soutullo, C. A. (2017). Weight, height, and body mass index in patients with attention-deficit/hyperactivity disorder treated with methylphenidate. *Journal of Child and Adolescent Psychopharmacology, 27*(8), 723–730.

Dillon, A., & Craven, R. G. (2014). Examining the genetic contribution to ADHD. *Ethical Human Psychology & Psychiatry, 16*(1), 20–28.

Domingues-Montanari, S. (2017). Clinical and psychological effects of excessive screen time on children. *Journal of Paediatrics and Child Health, 53*(4), 333–338.

Draper, S. (2012). *Out of my mind*. Atheneum.

Duh-Leong, C., Fuller, A., & Brown, N. M. (2020). Associations between family and community protective factors and attention-deficit/hyperactivity disorder outcomes among US children. *Journal of Developmental & Behavioral Pediatrics, 41*(1), 1–8.

Durand, V. M., & Crimmins, D. B. (1988). Identifying the variables maintaining self-injurious behavior. *Journal of Autism and Developmental Disorders, 18*(1), 99–117.

Durand, V. M., & Crimmins, D. B. (1992). *The Motivation Assessment Scale (MAS) administration guide*. Monaco and Associates.

Education for All Handicapped Children Act of 1975, Public Law No. 94-142. 89 Stat. 773.

Edwards, C., Howlett, E., Akrich, M., & Rabeharisoa, V. (2014). Attention deficit hyperactivity disorder in France and Ireland: Parents' groups' scientific and political framing of an unsettled condition. *BioSocieties, 9*, 153–172.

Engle, R. W. (2018). Working memory and executive attention: A revisit. *Perspectives on Psychological Science, 13*(2), 190–193.

Epstein, J. N., & Loren, R. E. (2013). Changes in the definition of ADHD in DSM-5: Subtle but important. *Neuropsychiatry, 3*(5), 455.

Erlandsson, S., Lundin, L., & Punzi, E. (2016). A discursive analysis concerning information on "ADHD" presented to parents by the National Institute of Mental Health (USA). *International Journal of Qualitative Studies on Health and Well-being, 11*(1), 30938.

Evans, S., Owens, J., & Bunford, N. (2014). Evidence-based psychosocial treatments for children and adolescents with attention-deficit/hyperactivity disorder. *Journal of Clinical Child & Adolescent Psychology, 43*(4), 527–551.

Evans, S. W., Owens, J. S., Wymbs, B. T., & Ray, A. R. (2018). Evidence-based psychosocial treatments for children and adolescents with attention deficit/hyperactivity disorder. *Journal of Clinical Child & Adolescent Psychology, 47*(2), 157–198.

Ewe, L. P. (2019). ADHD symptoms and the teacher–student relationship: A systematic literature review. *Emotional and Behavioural Difficulties, 24*(2), 136–155.

Fadus, M. C., Ginsburg, K. R., Sobowale, K., Halliday-Boykins, C. A., Bryant, B. E., Gray, K. M., & Squeglia, L. M. (2020). Unconscious bias and the diagnosis of disruptive behavior disorders and ADHD in African American and Hispanic youth. *Academic Psychiatry, 44*, 95–102.

Faraone, S. V., Banaschewski, T., Coghill, D., Zheng, Y., Biederman, J., Bellgrove, M. A., Newcorn, J. H., Gignac, M., Al Saud, N. M., Manor, I., Rohde, L. A., Yang, L., Cortese, S., Almagor, D., Stein, M. A., Albatti, T. H., Aljoudi, H. F., Alqahtani, M. M. J., Asherson, P., … & Wang, Y. (2021). The world federation of ADHD international consensus statement: 208 evidence-based conclusions about the disorder. *Neuroscience & Biobehavioral Reviews, 128*, 789–818.

Fay, J., & Funk, D. (1995). *Teaching with love and logic: Taking control of the classroom.* Love and Logic Press.

Fisher, A. V., Godwin, K. E., & Seltman, H. (2014). Visual environment, attention allocation, and learning in young children: When too much of a good thing may be bad. *Psychological Science, 25*(7), 1362–1370.

Flavell, J. H. (1979). Metacognition and cognitive monitoring: A new area of cognitive–developmental inquiry. *American Psychologist, 34*(10), 906.

Fletcher, A. (2002). *FireStarter Youth Power curriculum: Participant guidebook.* Freechild Project.

Food and Drug Administration (FDA). (2021). Drugs@FDA: FDA-approved drugs. https://www.accessdata.fda.gov/scripts/cder/daf/index.cfm?event=reportsSearch. process&rptName=1&reportSelectMonth=12&reportSelectYear=1955&nav

Fortenbaugh, F. C., DeGutis, J., & Esterman, M. (2017). Recent theoretical, neural, and clinical advances in sustained attention research. *Annals of the New York Academy of Sciences, 1396*(1), 70–91.

Freire, P. (1970). *Pedagogy of the oppressed.* Seabury.

Garcia, J. (2013). Using similes to check for understanding. [Video]. YouTube. https://www.youtube.com/watch?v=Ylg3olrF5eY

Gardner, H. (1983). *Frames of mind: The theory of multiple intelligences.* Basic Books.

Gardner, H. (2011). *Frames of mind: The theory of multiple intelligences* (3rd ed.) Basic Books.

Garnock-Jones, K. P., & Keating, G. M. (2009). Atomoxetine: A review of its use in attention-deficit hyperactivity disorder in children and adolescents. *Paediatric Drugs, 11*, 203–226.

Gay, G. (2018). *Culturally responsive teaching: Theory, research, and practice* (3rd ed.). Teachers College Press.

Gazzaley, A., & D'Esposito, M. (2007). Unifying prefrontal cortex function: Executive control, neural networks and top-down modulation. In J. Cummings & B. Miller (Eds.), *The human frontal lobes* (2nd ed.) (pp. 187–206). Guilford.

Gill, P., & Remedios, R. (2013). How should researchers in education operationalise on-task behaviours? *Cambridge Journal of Education, 43*(2), 199–222.

Gioia, G. A., Isquith, P. K., Guy, S. C., & Kenworthy, L. (2000). *BRIEF: Behavior Rating Inventory of Executive Function.* Psychological Assessment Resources.

Godwin, K. E., Almeda, M. V., Petroccia, M., Baker, R. S., & Fisher, A. V. (2013). Classroom activities and off-task behavior in elementary school children. *Proceedings of the Annual Meeting of the Cognitive Science Society, 35*(35), 2428–2433.

Godwin, K. E., Almeda, M. V., Seltman, H., Kai, S., Skerbetz, M. D., Baker, R. S., & Fisher, A. V. (2016). Off-task behavior in elementary school children. *Learning and Instruction, 44*, 128–143.

GoNoodle. (2016, October 5). Trolls: Can't stop the feeling [Video]. https://www.youtube.com/watch?v=KhfkYzUwYFk

González, N., Moll, L. C., & Amanti, C. (2005). *Funds of knowledge: Theorizing practices in households, communities, and classrooms.* Lawrence Erlbaum Associates.

Goodwin, M. (2010). *On the other side of hyperactivity: An anthropology of ADHD* (Doctoral dissertation, University of California–Berkeley).

Gordon, W. J. (1961). *Synectics: The development of creative capacity.* Harper & Row.

Gragg, S., & Collet, V. (2023). The impact of a relationship-building strategy on teachers' perceptions of preschooler behavior: A 2 X 10 approach. *Early Years, 43*(1), 182–196.

Greenwald, A. G., Rudman, L. A., Nosek, B. A., Banaji, M. R., Farnham, S. D., & Mellot, D. S. (2002). A unified theory of implicit attitudes, stereotypes, self-esteem and self-concept. *Psychological Review, 109*(1), 3–25

Grenny, J., Patterson, K., McMillan, R., Switzler, A., & Gregory, E. (2022). *Crucial conversations: Tools for talking when stakes are high* (3rd ed.). McGraw-Hill Education.

Gross, J. (2019, November 16). The 50 best non-superhero graphic novels. *Rolling Stone*. https://www.rollingstone.com/tv-movies/tv-movie-lists/drawn-out-the-50-best-non-superhero-graphic-novels-29579/

Gualtieri, C. T., & Johnson, L. G. (2008). Medications do not necessarily normalize cognition in ADHD patients. *Journal of Attention Disorders, 11*(4), 459–469.

Guthrie, J. T., Klauda, S. L., & Morrison, D. A. (2012). Motivation, achievement, and classroom contexts for information book reading. In J. T. Guthrie, A. Wigfield, & S. L. Klauda (Eds.), *Adolescents' engagement in academic literacy* (pp. 1–51). University of Maryland, Department of Human Development and Quantitative Methodology.

Hai, T., & Climie, E. A. (2022). Positive child personality factors in children with ADHD. *Journal of Attention Disorders, 26*(3), 476–486.

Haim, A. (2002). *The analysis and validation of the Motivation Assessment Scale-II Test Version: A structural equation model*. State University of New York–Albany.

Hajar, M. S., Rizal, H., & Kuan, G. (2019). Effects of physical activity on sustained attention: A systematic review. *Scientia Medica, 29*(2), e32864–e32864.

Harrison, J. R., Bunford, N., Evans, S. W., & Owens, J. S. (2013). Educational accommodations for students with behavioral challenges: A systematic review of the literature. *Review of Educational Research, 83*(4), 551–597.

Harrison, J. R., Evans, S. W., Baran, A., Khondker, F., Press, K., Noel, D., Wasserman, S., Belmonte, C., & Mohlmann, M. (2020). Comparison of accommodations and interventions for youth with ADHD: A randomized controlled trial. *Journal of School Psychology, 80*, 15–36.

Hattie, J. (2012). *Visible learning for teachers: Maximizing impact on learning*. Routledge.

Hattie, J., & Timperley, H. (2007). The power of feedback. *Review of educational research, 77*(1), 81–112.

Haynes, A. B., Weiser, T. G., Berry, W. R., Lipsitz, S. R., Breizat, A. H. S., Dellinger, E. P., … & Gawande, A. A. (2009). A surgical safety checklist to reduce morbidity and mortality in a global population. *New England Journal of Medicine, 360*(5), 491–499.

Hill, K. (2011). *The effects of graphic novels on the reading comprehension scores of students with autism spectrum disorders* (ASD). [Doctoral dissertation, University of Wisconsin–Superior].

Hinshaw, S. P. (2018). Attention deficit hyperactivity disorder (ADHD): Controversy, developmental mechanisms, and multiple levels of analysis. *Annual Review of Clinical Psychology, 14*, 291–316.

Hofer, M. (2007). Goal conflicts and self-regulation: A new look at pupils' off-task behaviour in the classroom. *Educational Research Review, 2*(1), 28–38.

Hommel, B., Chapman, C. S., Cisek, P., Neyedli, H. F., Song, J. H., & Welsh, T. N. (2019). No one knows what attention is. *Attention, Perception, & Psychophysics, 81*, 2288–2303.

Howard, T. (2003). Culturally relevant pedagogy: Ingredients for critical teacher reflection. *Theory into Practice, 42*(3), 195–202.

Howard, T., & Terry Sr., C. L. (2011). Culturally responsive pedagogy for African American students: Promising programs and practices for enhanced academic performance. *Teaching Education, 22*(4), 345–362.

Hoy, A. W., & Weinstein, C. S. (2013). Student and teacher perspectives on classroom management. In C. M. Evertson & C. S. Weinstein (Eds.), *Handbook of classroom management: Research, practice, and contemporary issues* (pp. 181–220). Routledge.

Hua, M. H., Huang, K. L., Hsu, J. W., Bai, Y. M., Su, T. P., Tsai, S. J., Li, C. T., Lin, W. C., Chen, T. J., & Chen, M. H. (2021). Early pregnancy risk among adolescents with ADHD: A nationwide longitudinal study. *Journal of Attention Disorders, 25*(9), 1199–1206.

Huang, K. L., Wei, H. T., Hsu, J. W., Bai, Y. M., Su, T. P., Li, C. T., Lin, W. C., Tsai, S. J., Chang, W. H., Chen, T. J., & Chen, M. H. (2018). Risk of suicide attempts in adolescents and young adults with attention-deficit hyperactivity disorder: A nationwide longitudinal study. *British Journal of Psychiatry, 212*(4), 234–238.

Hustus, C. L., Evans, S. W., Sarno Owens, J., Benson, K., Hetrick, A. A., Kipperman, K., & DuPaul, G. J. (2020). An evaluation of 504 and individualized education programs for high school students with attention deficit hyperactivity disorder. *School Psychology Review, 49*(3), 333–345.

Individuals with Disabilities Education Improvement Act of 2004 (IDEA), 20 U.S.C. § 1400 et seq.

Iwata, B. A., Dorsey, M. F., Slifer, K. J., Bauman, K. E., & Richman, G. S. (1982). Toward a functional analysis of self-injury. *Analysis and Intervention in Developmental Disabilities, 2*, 3–20.

Iwata, B. A., Dorsey, M. F., Slifer, K. J., Bauman, K. E., & Richman, G. S. (1994). Toward a functional analysis of self-injury. *Journal of Applied Behavior Analysis, 27*(2), 197–209.

James, W. (1890). *The principles of psychology* (Vol. 1). Henry Holt.

Jensen, P. S., & Kenny, D. T. (2004). The effects of yoga on the attention and behavior of boys with attention-deficit/hyperactivity disorder (ADHD). *Journal of Attention Disorders, 7*(4), 205–216.

Kaefer, T. (2018). The role of topic-related background knowledge in visual attention to illustration and children's word learning during shared book reading. *Journal of Research in Reading, 41*(3), 582–596.

Kaefer, T. (2020). When did you learn it? How background knowledge impacts attention and comprehension in read-aloud activities. *Reading Research Quarterly, 55*, S173–S183.

Kagan, S. (1989). The structural approach to cooperative learning. *Educational Leadership, 47*(4), 12–15.

Kahn, E., & Cohen, L. H. (1934). Organic drivenness: A brain-stem syndrome and an experience. *New England Journal of Medicine, 210*, 748–756.

Kazda, L., Bell, K., Thomas, R., McGeechan, K., Sims, R., & Barratt, A. (2021). Overdiagnosis of attention-deficit/hyperactivity disorder in children and adolescents: A systematic scoping review. *JAMA Network Open, 4*(4), e215335–e215335.

Keller, A. S., Davidesco, I., & Tanner, K. D. (2020). Attention matters: How orchestrating attention may relate to classroom learning [Special online issue]. *CBE Life Sciences Education, 19*(3).

Kiat, J. E., Cheadle, J. E., & Goosby, B. J. (2018). The impact of social exclusion on anticipatory attentional processing. *International Journal of Psychophysiology, 123*, 48–57.

Kiboomers. (2015, March 25). Party freeze dance song: The Kiboomers preschool songs for circle time [Video]. https://www.youtube.com/watch?v=2UcZWXvgMZE

Kilian, B., Hofer, M., Fries, S., & Kuhnle, C. (2010). The conflict between on-task and off-task actions in the classroom and its consequences for motivation and achievement. *European Journal of Psychology of Education, 25*(1), 67–85.

Kim, J. W., Lee, Y. S., Han, D. H., Min, K. J., Kim, D. H., & Lee, C. W. (2015). The utility of quantitative electroencephalography and integrated visual and auditory continuous performance test as auxiliary tools for the attention deficit hyperactivity disorder diagnosis. *Clinical Neurophysiology, 126*(3), 532–540.

Kim, S., & Rehder, B. (2011). How prior knowledge affects selective attention during category learning: An eyetracking study. *Memory and Cognition, 39*, 649–665.

Kincade, L., Cook, C., & Goerdt, A. (2020). Meta-analysis and common practice elements of universal approaches to improving student-teacher relationships. *Review of Educational Research, 90*(5), 710–748

Kintsch, W. (1998). *Comprehension: A paradigm for cognition.* Cambridge University Press.

Koelewijn, T., Bronkhorst, A. W., & Theeuwes, J. (2010). Attention and the multiple stages of multisensory integration: A review of audiovisual studies. *Acta Psychologica, 134*(3), 372–384.

Kofler, M. J., Rapport, M. D., Sarver, D. E., Raiker, J. S., Orban, S. A., Friedman, L. M., & Kolomeyer, E. G. (2013). Reaction time variability in ADHD: A meta-analytic review of 319 studies. *Clinical Psychology Review, 33*(6), 795–811.

Kohli, R., & Solórzano, D. G. (2012). Teachers, please learn our names! Racial microaggressions and the K–12 classroom. *Race Ethnicity and Education, 15*(4), 441–462.

Konrad, M., Joseph, L. M., & Eveleigh, E. (2009). A meta-analytic review of guided notes. *Education and Treatment of Children, 32*, 421–444.

Koutsoklenis, A., & Honkasilta, J. (2023). ADHD in the DSM-5-TR: What has changed and what has not. *Frontiers in Psychiatry, 13*, 1064141, 1–26.

Krauzlis, R. J., Bollimunta, A., Arcizet, F., & Wang, L. (2014). Attention as an effect not a cause. *Trends in Cognitive Sciences, 18*(9), 457–464.

Kruger, A., & DeNisi, A. (1996). The effects of feedback interventions on performance: An historical review, meta-analysis and preliminary feedback theory. *Psychological Bulletin, 119*, 254–285.

Ladson-Billings, G. J. (1997). *The dreamkeepers: Successful teachers of African-American children.* Jossey-Bass.

Lambert, T. (2003). Visual orienting, learning and conscious awareness. *Attention and Implicit Learning, 48*, 253–276.

Lankshear, C., & Knobel, M. (2003). *New literacies: Changing knowledge and classroom learning.* Open University Press.

Lantieri, L. (2008). Nurturing inner calm in children. *Encounter, 21*(3), 32–37.

Lasko, B. (2020). The importance of relationship building with ADHD students. *BU Journal of Graduate Studies in Education, 12*(2), 29–32.

Laufer, M. W., Denhoff, E., & Solomons, G. (1957). Hyperkinetic impulse disorder in children's behavior problems. *Psychosomatic Medicine, 19*, 38–49.

Lavie, N. (1995). Perceptual load as a necessary condition for selective attention. *Journal of Experimental Psychology: Human Perception and Performance, 21*, 451–468.

Lavie, N., Hirst, A., De Fockert, J. W., & Viding, E. (2004). Load theory of selective attention and cognitive control. *Journal of Experimental Psychology: General, 133*(3), 339–354.

Lissak, G. (2018). Adverse physiological and psychological effects of screen time on children and adolescents: Literature review and case study. *Environmental Research, 164*, 149–157.

López, F. A. (2017). Altering the trajectory of the self-fulfilling prophecy: Asset-based pedagogy and classroom dynamics. *Journal of Teacher Education, 1*(2), 193.

Lovett, B. J., & Nelson, J. M. (2021). Systematic review: Educational accommodations for children and adolescents with attention-deficit/hyperactivity disorder. *Journal of the American Academy of Child & Adolescent Psychiatry, 60*(4), 448–457.

Luman, M., Oosterlaan, J., & Sergeant, J. A. (2008). Modulation of response timing in ADHD, effects of reinforcement valence and magnitude. *Journal of Abnormal Child Psychology, 36*(3), 445–456.

Luna, B. (2009). Developmental changes in cognitive control through adolescence. *Advances in Child Development and Behavior, 37*, 233–278.

Luo, Y., Weibman, D., Halperin, J. M., & Li, X. (2019). A review of heterogeneity in attention deficit/hyperactivity disorder (ADHD). *Frontiers in Human Neuroscience, 13*, 42.

Lyman, F. (1981). The responsive classroom discussion. In A. S. Anderson (Ed.), *Mainstreaming digest* (pp. 109–113). University of Maryland College of Education.

Ma, J. K., Le Mare, L., & Gurd, B. J. (2015, March). Four minutes of in-class high-intensity interval activity improves selective attention in 9- to 11-year-olds. *Applied Physiology, Nutrition, and Metabolism, 40*(3), 238–244.

Malmberg, K. J., Raaijmakers, J. G. W., & Shiffrin, R. M. (2019). 50 years of research sparked by Atkinson and Shiffrin (1968). *Memory & Cognition, 47*(4), 561–574.

Manzo, A. V. (1969). *Improving reading comprehension through reciprocal questioning*. Syracuse University.

Manzo, A. V. (1970). Reading and questioning: The ReQuest procedure. *Reading Improvement, 7*(3), 80.

March, R. E., Horner, R. H., Lewis-Palmer, T., Brown, D., Crone, D., & Todd, A. W.(2000). Functional assessment checklist: Teachers and staff (FACTS). Educational and Community Supports.

Marsh, J. E., Campbell, T. A., Vachon, F., Taylor, P. J., & Hughes, R. W. (2020, January). How the deployment of visual attention modulates auditory distraction. *Attention, Perception & Psychophysics, 82*(1), 350–362.

Martinez-Cedillo, A. P., Dent, K., & Foulsham, T. (2022). Do cognitive load and ADHD traits affect the tendency to prioritise social information in scenes? *Quarterly Journal of Experimental Psychology, 75*(10), 1904–1918.

Marton, I., Wiener, J., Rogers, M., Moore, C., & Tannock, R. (2009). Empathy and social perspective taking in children with attention-deficit/hyperactivity disorder. *Journal of Abnormal Child Psychology, 37*(1), 107–118.

Marx, I., Cortese, S., Koelch, M. G., & Hacker, T. (2022). Meta-analysis: Altered perceptual timing abilities in attention-deficit/hyperactivity disorder. *Journal of the American Academy of Child & Adolescent Psychiatry, 61*(7), 866–880.

Marzano, R. J. (1998). *A theory-based meta-analysis of research on instruction*. Mid-continent Research for Education and Learning.

Mavilidi, M., Ouwehand, K., Okely, A. D., Chandler, P., & Paas, F. (2019). Embodying learning through physical activity and gestures in preschool children. In S. Tindall-Ford, S. Agostinho, & J. Sweller (Eds.), *Advances in cognitive load theory* (pp. 103–118). Routledge.

Mayer, R. E., Mathias, A., & Wetzell, K. (2002). Fostering understanding of multimedia messages through pre-training: Evidence for a two-stage theory of mental model construction. *Journal of Experimental Psychology: Applied, 8*(3), 147–154.

Mayes, R., & Rafalovich, A. (2007, December). Suffer the restless children: The evolution of ADHD and paediatric stimulant use, 1900–80. *History of Psychiatry, 18*(72, Pt. 4), 435–457.

McKibben, S. (2014). The two-minute relationship builder. *Education Update, 56*(7), 2–3.

Mehta, S., Mehta, V., Mehta, S., Shah, D., Motiwala, A., Vardhan, J., Mehta, N., & Mehta, D. (2011). Multimodal behavior program for ADHD incorporating yoga and implemented by high school volunteers: A pilot study. *International Scholarly Research Notices, 2011*, 780745.

Microsoft. (2015). *Attention spans*. Consumer Insights, Microsoft Canada.

Mikami, A. Y., Smit, S., & Johnston, C. (2019). Teacher attributions for children's attention deficit/hyperactivity disorder behaviours predict experiences with children and with classroom behavioural management in a summer program practicum. *Psychology in the Schools, 56*(6), 928–944.

Mikkonen, K., & Lautenbacher, O. P. (2019). Global attention in reading comics: Eye movement indications of interplay between narrative content and layout. *ImageTexT, 10*(2).

Mitchell, J., & Read, J. (2011). Attention-deficit hyperactivity disorder, drug companies and the Internet. *Clinical Child Psychology and Psychiatry, 17*(1), 121–139.

Molina, B. S. G., Hinshaw, S. P., Swanson, J. M., Arnold, L. E., Vitiello, B., Jensen, P. S., Epstein, J. N., Hoza, B., Hechtman, L., Abikoff, H. B., Elliott, G. R., Greenhill, L. L., Newcorn, J. H., Wells, K. C., Wigal, T., Gibbons, R. D., Hur, K., Houck, P. R., & MTA Cooperative Group. (2009). The MTA at 8 years: Prospective follow-up of children treated for combined-type ADHD in a multisite study. *Journal of the American Academy of Child and Adolescent Psychiatry, 48*(5), 484–500.

Moll, L. C., Amanti, C., Neff, D., & González, N. (1992). Funds of knowledge for teaching: using a qualitative approach to connect homes and classrooms. *Theory into Practice, 31*(2), 132–141.

Montalva-Valenzuela, F., Andrades-Ramírez, O., & Castillo-Paredes, A. (2022). Effects of physical activity, exercise and sport on executive function in young people with attention deficit hyperactivity disorder: a systematic review. *European Journal of Investigation in Health, Psychology and Education, 12*(1), 61–76.

Moore, D., Russell, A., Matthews, J., Ford, T., Rogers, M., Ukoumunne, O. C., Kneale, D., Thompson Coon, J., Sutcliffe, K., Nunns, M., Shaw, L., & Gwernan-Jones, R. (2018). School-based interventions for attention-deficit/hyperactivity disorder: A systematic review with multiple synthesis methods. *Review of Education, 6*(3), 209–263.

Moray, N. P. (1959). Attention in dichotic listening: Affective cues and the influence of instructions. *Quarterly Journal of Experimental Psychology, 11*(1), 56–60.

Morgan, H. (1996). An analysis of Gardner's theory of multiple intelligence. *Roeper Review, A Journal on Gifted Education, 18*(4), 263–269.

Mueller, A., Hong, D. S., Shepard, S., & Moore, T. (2017). Linking ADHD to the neural circuitry of attention. *Trends in Cognitive Sciences, 21*(6), 474–488.

Mueller, A. K., Fuermaier, A. B., Koerts, J., & Tucha, L. (2012). Stigma in attention deficit hyperactivity disorder. *ADHD Attention Deficit and Hyperactivity Disorders, 4*(3), 101–114.

Mulqueeny, K., Kostyuk, V., Baker, R. S., & Ocumpaugh, J. (2015). Incorporating effective e-learning principles to improve student engagement in middle-school mathematics. *International Journal of STEM Education, 2*(15).

Murray, A. L., Hall, H. A., Speyer, L. G., Carter, L., Mirman, D., Caye, A., & Rohde, L. (2022). Developmental trajectories of ADHD symptoms in a large population-representative longitudinal study. *Psychological Medicine, 52*(15), 3590–3596.

National Academies of Sciences, Engineering, and Medicine. (2018). *How people learn II: Learners, contexts, and cultures*. National Academies Press.

National Institute of Mental Health (NIMH). (2009). *About RDoC*. https://www.nimh.nih.gov/research/research-funded-by-nimh/rdoc/about-rdoc

National Institute of Mental Health (NIMH). (2019). *Attention-Deficit/Hyperactivity Disorder*. https://www.nimh.nih.gov/health/topics/attention-deficit-hyperactivity-disorder-adhd

Neiman, B., Cohen Harper, J., & Lewis, S. (2015). *My calm place: Yoga and mindfulness practices for children card deck*. Pesi.

Nelson, J. R., Roberts, M., & Smith, D. J. (1998). *Conducting functional behavioral assessments in school settings: A practical guide*. Sopris West.

Nigg, J. T., Karalunas, S. L., Feczko, E., & Fair, D. A. (2020). Toward a revised nosology for ADHD heterogeneity. *Biological Psychiatry: Cognitive Neuroscience and Neuroimaging, 5*(8), 726.

Ogle, D. M. (1986). K-W-L: A teaching model that develops active reading of expository text. *The Reading Teacher, 39*(6), 564–570.

Ohno, T. (1978). *Toyota production system: Beyond large-scale production*. Diamond. (Original Japanese version)

Ohno, T. (1988). *Toyota production system: Beyond large-scale production*. Productivity Press.

Oken, B. S., Salinsky, M. C., & Elsas, S. M. (2006). Vigilance, alertness, or sustained attention: Physiological basis and measurement. *Clinical Neurophysiology, 117*(9), 1885–1901.

Palincsar, A. S., & Brown, A. L. (1984). Reciprocal teaching of comprehension-fostering and comprehension-monitoring activities. *Cognition and Instruction, 1*(2), 117–175.

Pallini, S., Vecchio, G. M., Baiocco, R., Schneider, B. H., & Laghi, F. (2019). Student–teacher relationships and attention problems in school-aged children: The mediating role of emotion regulation. *School Mental Health, 11*, 309–320.

Palmer, P. J. (1997). *The courage to teach: Exploring the inner landscape of a teacher's life.* Jossey-Bass.

Palmer, P. J. (2017). *The courage to teach: Exploring the inner landscape of a teacher's life, 20th anniversary edition.* Wiley.

Palomares, I., Martínez, L., & Herrera, F. (2014). A consensus model to detect and manage noncooperative behaviors in large-scale group decision making. In *IEEE Transactions on Fuzzy Systems, 22*(3), 516–530.

Parker, D. R., Hoffman, S. F., Sawilowsky, S., & Rolands, L. (2011). An examination of the effects of ADHD coaching on university students' executive functioning. *Journal of Postsecondary Education and Disability, 24*(2), 115–132.

Pashler, H. (1997). *The psychology of attention.* MIT Press.

Pashler, H., McDaniel, M., Rohrer, D., & Bjork, R. (2008). Learning styles: Concepts and evidence. *Psychological Science in the Public Interest, 9*(3), 105–119.

Patrick, K., Socol, A., & Morgan, I. (2020). *Inequities in advanced coursework: What's driving them and what leaders can do.* Education Trust.

Pearson, P. D., & Gallagher, M. C. (1983). The instruction of reading comprehension. *Contemporary Educational Psychology, 8*(3), 317–344.

Pereira, A., Miranda, S., Teixeira, S., Mesquita, S., Zanatta, C., & Rosário, P. (2021, March 1). Promote selective attention in 4th-grade students: Lessons learned from a school-based intervention on self-regulation. *Children, 8*(3), 182.

Pérez-Álvarez, M. (2017). The four causes of ADHD: Aristotle in the classroom. *Frontiers in Psychology, 8*, 928.

Petersen, S. E., & Posner, M. I. (2012). The attention system of the human brain: 20 years after. *Annual Review of Neuroscience, 35*, 73–89.

Piaget, J. (1952). *The origins of intelligence in children.* International Universities Press.

Piaget, J. (1954). *The construction of reality in the child.* Basic Books.

Ponce, H. R., & Mayer, R. E. (2014). An eye movement analysis of highlighting and graphic organizer study aids for learning from expository text. *Computers in Human Behavior, 41*, 21–32.

Posner, J., Russell, J. A., & Peterson, B. S. (2005). The circumplex model of affect: An integrative approach to affective neuroscience, cognitive development, and psychopathology. *Development and Psychopathology, 17*(3), 715–734.

Posner, M. I. (1980). Orienting of attention. *Quarterly Journal of Experimental Psychology, 32*(1), 3–25.

Posner, M. I. (2023). The evolution and future development of attention networks. *Journal of Intelligence, 11*(6), 98.

Posner, M. I., & Petersen, S. E. (1990). The attention system of the human brain. *Annual Review of Neuroscience, 13*, 25–42.

Posner M. I., Petersen S. E., Fox P. T., & Raichle, M. E. (1988, June). Localization of cognitive operations in the human brain. *Science, 240*(4859), 1627–1631.

Posner, M. I., & Rothbart, M. K. (2007). *Educating the human brain.* American Psychological Association Books.

Posner, M. I., & Rothbart, M. K. (2009). Toward a physical basis of attention and self regulation. *Physics of Life Reviews, 6*(2), 103.

Posner, M. I., & Rothbart, M. K. (2018, April 19). Temperament and brain networks of attention. *Philosophical Transactions of the Royal Society of London, Series B: Biological Sciences, 373*(1744), 20170254.

Posner, M. I., & Rothbart, M. K. (2023). Fifty years integrating neurobiology and psychology to study attention. *Biological Psychology, 180*(9), 108574.

Posner, M. I., Rothbart, M. K., & Ghassemzadeh, H. (2019). Restoring attention networks. *Yale Journal of Biology and Medicine, 92*(1), 139–143.

Posner, M. I., Rothbart, M. K., & Voelker, P. (2016). Developing brain networks of attention. *Current Opinion in Pediatrics, 28*(6), 720.

Powell, S. G., Frydenberg, M., & Thomsen, P. H. (2015). The effects of long-term medication on growth in children and adolescents with ADHD: An observational study of a large cohort of real-life patients. *Child and Adolescent Psychiatry and Mental Health, 9*(1), 1–13.

Prezi. (2018). *2018 state of attention.* https://prezi.com/p/nsquynpwsvwx/2018-state-of-attention-us-edition/

Prichard, C., & Atkins, A. (2019). Selective attention of L2 learners in task-based reading online. *Reading in a Foreign Language, 31*(2), 269–290.

Quinn, D. M. (2017). Racial attitudes of preK–12 and postsecondary educators: Descriptive evidence from nationally representative data. *Educational Researcher, 46*(7), 397–411.

Quinn, D. M., & Stewart, A. M. (2019). Examining the racial attitudes of white pre-K–12 teachers. *Elementary School Journal, 120*(2), 272–299.

Rehabilitation Act of 1973, Public Law No. 93-112, Sec. 504.

Reid, R., Trout, A. L., & Schartz, M. (2005). Self-regulation interventions for children with attention deficit/hyperactivity disorder. *Exceptional Children, 71*(4), 361–377.

Ribeiro, J. P., Lunde, C., Gluud, C., Simonsen, E., & Storebø, O. J. (2023). Methylphenidate denied access to the WHO List of Essential Medicines for the second time. *BMJ Evidence-Based Medicine, 28*(2), 75–77.

Richards, L. M. (2013). It is time for a more integrated bio-psycho-social approach to ADHD. *Clinical Child Psychology and Psychiatry, 18*(4), 483–503.

Riddle, M. A., Yershova, K., Lazzaretto, D., Paykina, N., Yenokyan, G., Greenhill, L., Abikoff, H., Vitiello, B., Wigal, T., McCracken, J. T., Kollins, S. H., Murray, D. W., Wigal, S., Kastelic, E., McGough, J. J., dosReis, S., Bauzó-Rosario, A., Stehli, A., & Posner, K. (2013, March). The preschool attention-deficit/hyperactivity disorder treatment study (PATS) 6-year follow-up. *Journal of the American Academy of Child & Adolescent Psychiatry, 52*(3), 264–278.

Robertson, I. H., Manly, T., Andrade, J., Baddeley, B. T., & Yiend, J. (1997). "Oops!" Performance correlates of everyday attentional failures in traumatic brain injured and normal subjects. *Neuropsychologia, 35*(6), 747–758.

Robinson, F. P. (1941). *Diagnostic and remedial techniques for effective study.* Harper.

Robinson, K. (2006, February). *Do schools kill creativity?* [Video]. TED Talk. https://www.ted.com/talks/sir_ken_robinson_do_schools_kill_creativity?hasSummary=true&language=en

Rogers, M., Bélanger-Lejars, V., Toste, J. R., & Heath, N. L. (2015). Mismatched: ADHD symptomatology and the teacher-student relationship. *Emotional and Behavioural Difficulties, 20*(4), 333–348.

Rogers, M., & Tannock, R. (2013). Are classrooms meeting the basic psychological needs of children with ADHD symptoms? A self-determination theory perspective. *Journal of Attention Disorders, 22*(14), 1354–1360.

Ross, L. (1977). The intuitive psychologist and his shortcomings: Distortions in the attribution process. In L. Berkowitz (Ed.), *Advances in experimental social psychology* (Vol. 10) (pp. 173–220). Academic Press.

Rothbart, M. K., & Jones, L. B. (1998). Temperament, self-regulation, and education. *School Psychology Review, 27*(4), 479–491.

Rothbart, M. K., & Posner, M. I. (2015). The developing brain in a multitasking world. *Developmental Review, 35*, 42–63.

Rothstein, D., & Santana, L. (2011). Teaching students to ask their own questions. *Harvard Education Letter, 27*(5), 1–2.

Rowland-Bryant, E., Skinner, C. H., Skinner, A. L., Saudargas, R., Robinson, D. H., & Kirk, E. R. (2009). Investigating the interaction of graphic organizers and seductive details: Can a graphic organizer mitigate the seductive-details effect? *Research in the Schools, 16*(2), 29-40.

Rueda, M. R., Fan, J., Halparin, J., Gruber, D., Lercari, L. P., McCandliss, B. D. & Posner, M. I. (2004). Development of attentional networks in childhood. *Neuropsychologia, 42*(8), 1029–1040.

Rueda, M. R., Posner, M. I., & Rothbart, M. K. (2004). Attentional control and self-regulation. *Handbook of Self-regulation: Research, Theory, and Applications, 2*, 284–299.

Ryan, R. M., & Deci, E. L. (2006). Self-regulation and the problem of human autonomy: Does psychology need choice, self-determination, and will? *Journal of Personality, 74*(6), 1557–1586.

Santos, R. M. S., Mendes, C. G., Marques Miranda, D., & Romano-Silva, M. A. (2022). The association between screen time and attention in children: A systematic review. *Developmental Neuropsychology, 47*(4), 175–192.

Saripah, I., & Widiastuti, H. T. (2019). Profile of off-task behavior in primary school students. *Mimbar Sekolah Dasar, 6*(2), 174–184.

Savickas, M. (2019). *Career counseling.* American Psychological Association.

Savickas, M. L., Brown, S. D., & Lent, R. W. (2005). The theory and practice of career construction. In S. D. Brown & R. W. Lent (Eds.), *Career development and counseling: Putting theory and research to work* (pp. 42–70). Wiley.

Sax, L., & Kautz, K. J. (2003). Who first suggests the diagnosis of attention-deficit/hyperactivity disorder? *Annals of Family Medicine, 1*(3), 171–174.

Sayal, K., Chudal, R., Hinkka-Yli-Salomäki, S., Joelsson, P., & Sourander, A. (2017). Relative age within the school year and diagnosis of attention-deficit hyperactivity disorder: A nationwide population-based study. *The Lancet Psychiatry, 4*(11), 868–875.

Schatz, N. K., Fabiano, G. A., Raiker, J. S., Hayes, T. B., & Pelham Jr., W. E. (2021). Twenty-year trends in elementary teachers' beliefs about best practices for students with ADHD. *School Psychology, 36*(4), 203–213.

Schwartz, K. (2016). *I wish my teacher knew: How one question can change everything for our kids.* Da Capo Lifelong Books.

Seiffer, B., Hautzinger, M., Ulrich, R., & Wolf, S. (2021). The efficacy of physical activity for children with attention deficit hyperactivity disorder: A meta-analysis of randomized controlled trials. *Journal of Attention Disorders, 26*(5), 656–673.

Seriki, V. D., & Brown, C. T. (2017). A dream deferred: A retrospective view of culturally relevant pedagogy. *Teachers College Record, 119*(1) 1–8.

Shanahan, T., Callison, K., Carriere, C., Duke, N. K., Pearson, P. D., Schatschneider, C., & Torgesen, J. (2010). *Improving reading comprehension in kindergarten through 3rd grade: IES Practice Guide* (NCEE 2010-4038). National Center for Education Evaluation and Regional Assistance, Institute of Education Sciences, U.S. Department of Education.

Shell, D. F., & Flowerday, T. (2019). Affordances and attention: Learning and culture. In K. A. Renninger & S. E. Hidi (Eds.), *The Cambridge handbook of motivation and learning* (pp. 759–782). Cambridge University Press.

Sherman, J., Rasmussen, C., & Baydala, L. (2008). The impact of teacher factors on achievement and behavioural outcomes of children with attention deficit/hyperactivity disorder (ADHD): A review of the literature. *Educational Research, 50*(4), 347–360.

Siegel, D. J., & Bryson, T. P. (2011). *The whole-brain child: 12 revolutionary strategies to nurture your child's developing mind.* Random House Digital.

Smith, G., Jongeling, B., Hartmann, P., & Russel, C. (2010, February 7). *Raine ADHD study: Long-term outcomes associated with stimulant medication in the treatment of ADHD in children.* Government of Western Australia, Department of Health. https://ww2.health.wa.gov.au/~/media/Files/Corporate/Reports-and-publications/PDF/MICADHD_Raine_ADHD_Study_report_022010.pdf

Sohlberg, M. M., & Mateer, C. A. (1989). *Introduction to cognitive rehabilitation: Theory and practice.* Guilford.

Sonuga-Barke, E. J., Becker, S. P., Bölte, S., Castellanos, F. X., Franke, B., Newcorn, J. H., Nigg, J. T., Rohde, L. A., & Simonoff, E. (2023). Annual research review: Perspectives on progress in ADHD science—from characterization to cause. *Journal of Child Psychology and Psychiatry, 64*(4), 506–532.

Sonuga-Barke, E., & Kostyrka-Allchorne, K. (2023). Editorial perspective: Attention-deficit/hyperactivity disorder viewed as neuro-divergence in the digital world. *Journal of Child Psychology and Psychiatry, 64*(6), 972–974.

Sonuga-Barke, E., & Thapar, A. (2021). The neurodiversity concept: Is it helpful for clinicians and scientists? *The Lancet Psychiatry, 8*(7), 559–561.

Stevens, C., Harn, B., Chard, D. J., Currin, J., Parisi, D., & Neville, H. (2013). Examining the role of attention and instruction in at-risk kindergarteners: Electrophysiological measures of selective auditory attention before and after an early literacy intervention. *Journal of Learning Disabilities, 46*(1), 73–86.

Still, G. (1902). Some abnormal psychical conditions in children: The Goulstonian lectures. *The Lancet, 159*(4103), 1077–1082. https://www.thelancet.com/journals/lancet/article/PIIS0140-6736(01)70022-0/fulltext

Storebø, O. J., & Gluud, C. (2021). Methylphenidate for ADHD rejected from the WHO Essential Medicines List due to uncertainties in benefit-harm profile. *BMJ Evidence-Based Medicine, 26*(4), 172–175.

Subramanian, K. R. (2018). Myth and mystery of shrinking attention span. *International Journal of Trend in Research and Development, 5*(1), 1–6.

Sugai, G., & Horner, R. H. (2009). Defining and describing school-wide positive behavior support. In W. Sailor, G. Dunlap, G. Sugai, & R. Horner (Eds.), *Handbook of positive behavior supports: Issues in clinical child psychology* (pp. 307–326). Springer.

Swanson, M. (1989). Advancement via individual determination: Project AVID. *Educational Leadership, 46*(5), 63–64.

Swanson, M. (2004). AVID and the college board as the model for secondary school redesign, including a K–12 articulated plan. *Access, 10*(2), 4–5.

Szczygieł, E., Zielonka, K., Mętel, S., & Golec, J. (2017, March 31). Musculo-skeletal and pulmonary effects of sitting position: A systematic review. *Annals of Agricultural and Environmental Medicine, 24*(1), 8–12.

Tang, S., & Patrick, M. E. (2018). Technology and interactive social media use among 8th and 10th graders in the U.S. and associations with homework and school grades. *Computers in Human Behavior, 86*, 34–44.

Tang, Y. -Y., & Posner, M. (2009). Attention training and attention state training. *Trends in Cognitive Sciences, 13*, 222–227.

te Meerman, S., Batstra, L., Grietens, H., & Frances, A. (2017). ADHD: A critical update for educational professionals. *International Journal of Qualitative Studies on Health and Well-Being, 12*, 1–7.

Tepperman, A. (2019, March 4). Fraction in action [Video]. Moving EDGEucation. https://www.youtube.com/watch?v=8TyC5ikOZJo

Toste, J. R., Bloom, E. L., & Heath, N. L. (2014). The differential role of classroom working alliance in predicting school-related outcomes for students with and without high-incidence disabilities. *Journal of Special Education, 48*(2), 135–148.

Toste, J. R., Heath, N. L., McDonald Connor, C., & Peng, P. (2015). Reconceptualizing teacher-student relationships: Applicability of the working alliance within classroom contexts. *Elementary School Journal, 116*(1), 30–48.

Treisman, A. (1964). Selective attention in man. *British Medical Bulletin, 20*, 12–16.

Tseng, C. I., Laubrock, J., & Bateman, J. A. (2021). The impact of multimodal cohesion on attention and interpretation in film. *Discourse, Context & Media, 44*, 100544.

U.S. Department of Education. (2004). *Individuals with Disabilities Education Act of 2004*, Sec. 300.8(c) (9). https://sites.ed.gov/idea/regs/b/a/300.8/c/9

Vandenbroucke, L., Spilt, J., Verschueren, K., Piccinin, C., & Baeyens, D. (2018). The classroom as a developmental context for cognitive development: A meta-analysis on the importance of teacher-student interactions for children's executive functions. *Review of Educational Research, 88*(1), 125–164.

Venet, A. (2021, August 3). What I wish teachers knew about "what I wish my teacher knew." [Blog]. Unconditional Learning. https://www.unconditionallearning.org/blog/i-wish-teachers-knew

Visser, S. N., Danielson, M. L., Bitsko, R. H., Holbrook, J. R., Kogan, M. D., Ghandour, R. M., Perou, R., & Blumberg, S. J. (2014). Trends in the parent-report of health care provider-diagnosed and medicated attention-deficit/hyperactivity disorder: United States, 2003–2011. *Journal of the American Academy of Child & Adolescent Psychiatry, 53*(1), 34–46.

Vitiello, B., Elliott, G. R., Swanson, J. M., Arnold, L. E., Hechtman, L., Abikoff, H., Molina, B. S. G., Wells, K., Wigal, T., Jensen, P. S., Greenhill, L. L., Kaltman, J. R., Severe, J. B., Odbert, C., Hur, K., & Gibbons, R. (2012). Blood pressure and heart rate over 10 years in the multimodal treatment study of children with ADHD. *American Journal of Psychiatry, 169*(2), 167–177.

Vohs, K. D., & Baumeister, R. F. (Eds.). (2016). *Handbook of self-regulation: Research, theory, and applications*. Guilford.

Volkow, N. D., Wang, G. J., Fowler, J. S., Logan, J., Gerasimov, M., Maynard, L., Ding, Y. S., Gatley, S. J., Gifford, A., & Franceschi, D. (2001). Therapeutic doses of oral methylphenidate significantly increase extracellular dopamine in the human brain. *Journal of Neuroscience, 21*(2), RC121.

Volkow, N. D., Wang, G. J., Kollins, S. H., Wigal, T. L., Newcorn, J. H., Telang, F., Fowler, J. S., Zhu, W., Logan, J., Ma, Y., Pradhan, K., Wong, C., & Swanson, J. M. (2009). Evaluating dopamine reward pathway in ADHD: Clinical implications. *JAMA, 302*(10), 1084–1091.

Vygotsky, L. S. (1978). *Mind in society: Development of higher psychological processes*. Harvard University Press.

Walter, H. J., Gouze, K., & Lim, K. G. (2006). Teachers' beliefs about mental health needs in inner city elementary schools. *Journal of the American Academy of Child & Adolescent Psychiatry, 45*(1), 61–68.

Wang, H., & Hall, N. C. (2018). A systematic review of teachers' causal attributions: Prevalence, correlates, and consequences. *Frontiers in Psychology, 9*, 2305.

Wang, X., Mayer, R. E., Zhou, P., & Lin, L. (2021). Benefits of interactive graphic organizers in online learning: Evidence for generative learning theory. *Journal of Educational Psychology, 113*(5), 1024–1037.

Wang, X. L., Bernas, R., & Eberhard, P. (2004). Engaging ADHD students in tasks with hand gestures: A pedagogical possibility for teachers. *Educational Studies, 30*(3), 217–229.

Ward, S., & Jacobsen, K. (2014). A clinical model for developing executive function skills. *Perspectives on Language Learning and Education, 21*(2), 72–84.

Watson, T. S., Gresham, F. M., & Skinner, C. H. (2001). Introduction to the mini-series: Issues and procedures for implementing functional behavior assessments in schools. *School Psychology Review, 30*(2), 153–155.

Wechsler, D. (2014). *Wechsler intelligence scale for children* (5th ed.). The Psychological Corporation.

Wechsler, D. (2020). *Wechsler individual achievement test* (4th ed.). The Psychological Corporation.

Weldon, G., & Mayer, P. (2017). Let's get graphic: 100 favorite comics and graphic novels. *NPR.* https://www.npr.org/2017/07/12/533862948/lets-get-graphic-100-favorite-comics-and-graphic-novels

Wender, P. H., Epstein, R. S., Kopin, I. J., & Gordon, E. K. (1971). Urinary monoamine metabolites in children with minimal brain dysfunction. *American Journal of Psychiatry, 127*(10), 1411–1415.

Wenzel, J. M., Rauscher, N. A., Cheer, J. F., & Oleson, E. B. (2015, January). A role for phasic dopamine release within the nucleus accumbens in encoding aversion: A review of the neurochemical literature. *ACS Chemical Neuroscience, 6*(1), 16–26.

Westbrook, A., Van Den Bosch, R., Määttä, J. I., Hofmans, L., Papadopetraki, D., Cools, R., & Frank, M. J. (2020). Dopamine promotes cognitive effort by biasing the benefits versus costs of cognitive work. *Science, 367*(6484), 1362–1366.

Wienen, A. W., Sluiter, M. N., Thoutenhoofd, E., de Jonge, P., & Batstra, L. (2019). The advantages of an ADHD classification from the perspective of teachers. *European Journal of Special Needs Education, 34*(5), 649–662.

Wisniewski, B., Zierer, K., & Hattie, J. (2020). The power of feedback revisited: A meta-analysis of educational feedback research. *Frontiers in Psychology, 10*, 3087.

Wisniewski, R., Fawcett, G., Padak, N., & Rasinski, T. (2012). *Evidence-based instruction in reading: A professional development guide to culturally responsive instruction.* Pearson Education.

Witt, J. C., Daly, E. M., & Noell, G. (2000). *Functional assessments: A step-by-step guide to solving academic and behavior problems.* Sopris West.

Wodtke, G. T. (2012). The impact of education on intergroup attitudes: A multiracial analysis. *Social Psychology Quarterly, 75*(1), 80–106.

Xu, G., Strathearn, L., Liu, B., Yang, B., & Bao, W. (2018). Twenty-year trends in diagnosed attention-deficit/hyperactivity disorder among US children and adolescents, 1997–2016. *JAMA Network Open, 1*(4), e181471.

Xu, M., Li, Z., Diao, L., Fan, L., Zhang, L., Yuan, S., & Yang, D. (2017). Social exclusion impairs distractor suppression but not target enhancement in selective attention. *International Journal of Psychophysiology, 121*, 72–79.

Zhao, X., & Biernat, M. (2018). "I have two names, Xian and Alex": Psychological correlates of adopting Anglo names. *Journal of Cross-Cultural Psychology, 49*(4), 587–601.

Zwiers, J., & Crawford, M. (2009). How to start academic conversations. *Educational Leadership, 66*(7), 70–73.

Index

The letter *f* following a page locator denotes a figure.

About the Author

 **Dr. Robin Wisniewski** is a nationally certified school psychologist, licensed clinical psychologist, and past president of CO ASCD. She was lead author on *Evidence-Based Instruction in Reading: A Professional Development Guide to Culturally Responsive Instruction* and *Evidence-Based Instruction in Reading: A Professional Development Guide to Response to Intervention* (Pearson). Currently, she leads federally funded grants and state-level contracts as director of education systems improvement at RTI International.

Wisniewski's BA, BBA, MEd, EdS, and PhD are from Kent State University with a focus in curriculum and instruction, elementary through postsecondary literacy, and school psychology. While earning the PhD, she taught developmental education and led programs for students with learning and attention challenges.

Wisniewski earned tenure as an associate professor in teacher education and leadership at Baldwin Wallace University, having directed graduate programs in reading and higher education leadership. During her 30 years in education, she taught 132 course sections at four universities; conducted school, district, regional, and state-level systems improvement in 20 states and internationally; and directed administrative programs in reading and literacy, counseling, faculty development, and for students with disabilities.

About the Contributors

Nycole Bradshaw, MA, is senior manager of middle school mathematics at Denver School of Science and Technology in Denver, Colorado. Bradshaw has taught K–5 technology, 3rd grade, 5th grade, and middle school math during her 11 years as a teacher. Bradshaw believes that teaching and learning are reciprocal processes, every student brings something unique to the classroom, and students develop their potential when educators believe in them as capable individuals.

Marissa Coppock, MA, is a middle school social studies teacher at Colorado Early Colleges. Coppock has taught grades 4–12, as well as broad field social studies and English language arts during her eight years as a teacher. She is proud to have served the hineniteeno' (Northern Arapahoe People) on the Wind River Indian Reservation.

Sandra Golden, PhD, is director of diversity and the fellowships in equity and action at Hathaway Brown, an independent preK–12 all-girls school in Ohio. She has spent more than 20 years teaching preK through adulthood. Golden also has 25 years of experience in higher education, having earned tenure and full professorship, and has served in several administrative roles.

Ash Hall, MAT, is a special education teacher in Roaring Fork School District RE-1, Carbondale, Colorado. They have taught grades 1–8 and behavior intervention and special education during their seven years as a public school teacher. Hall has trained educators in multiple Colorado school districts in trauma-informed practices and behavior management.

Adrienne Hayes, MA, is a 5th grade teacher in Denver Public Schools, Colorado. Hayes has taught grades 3–5, including literacy, math, social studies, and science, as well as reading intervention for K–5 during her 11 years as a teacher. She has also served on the instructional leadership team, coaching and evaluating teachers within her school building.

Venessa Kayrell, BS, is national director of schools and partnerships at Cortica, a provider of therapies for children with autism and other developmental differences. Kayrell has taught math, physical sciences, and biological sciences in grades 6–12 during her 19 years in education. She also served as the head of school at Fusion Academy in Mission Viejo, California.

Seon Kim, BA, is assistant director of Fusion Academy in Mission Viejo, California, a personalized middle and high school. Kim has taught grades 1–12, primarily as a math and science teacher, during her 13 years of teaching. She has served as a math and science department head, as well as a national math department head for Fusion Academy schools.

Barbara Miller, MEd, is the emerging educators empowerment specialist at Lincoln Public Schools, Nebraska. Miller has taught general education for grades 4 and 5 and English language arts for grade 6 during her 35 years as a teacher. Miller is the 2015 recipient of the Florence J. Clark Award for Excellence in Middle School Teaching.

Sean Miller, MEd, MA, teaches social studies at South County High School in Fairfax County Public Schools, Virginia. He has taught grades 7–12, as well as African American history, AP African American studies, U.S. history, government, and English during his 10 years as a teacher. In 2021, Miller received George Washington's Mount Vernon History Teacher of the Year award, and in 2023, he received the Virginia Council for the Social Studies Civil Rights & Civil Liberties Excellence in Teaching award.

Liza Selvarajah, MA, CCC-SLP, is the founder and owner of Montreal Speech Therapy, an instructor at Fitchburg State University in Massachusetts, and a clinical educator at McGill University in Canada, specializing in supporting autistic students. Selvarajah taught K–1 deaf and hard-of-hearing students at Montreal Oral School and has taught high school, adult education, and college courses.

Danny Vương, MA, is a 5th grade teacher in Washington State, where he was his school board's 2019 Outstanding Educator of the Year. After switching from nursing to education, Vương taught 3rd, 4th, and in a 4th-5th grade split classroom, volunteered in 2nd grade, and substitute taught in K–12 during his first 10 years in education. He has also taught teacher professional development in Malaysia, and was a Vietnamese-English interpreter and a singer in the local Vietnamese community.

Kevin Wilson, MS, is a grade 6–12 teacher at Royal Live Oaks Academy of the Arts and Sciences in South Carolina. Wilson has taught grades K–12 art, served as a Positive Behavioral Interventions and Supports (PBIS) coach, and been a teacher mentor and evaluator. He has also coached various sports from youth to varsity, with basketball being his main sport during his 26 years as a teacher. He was selected Royal Live Oaks Academy of the Arts and Sciences High School Teacher of the Year in 2021–2022.

Related ASCD Resources: Attention

At the time of publication, the following resources were available (ASCD stock numbers in parentheses).

Building on the Strengths of Students with Special Needs: How to Move Beyond Disability Labels in the Classroom by Toby Karten (#117023)

Cultivating a Classroom of Calm: How to Promote Student Engagement and Self-Regulation by Meredith McNerney (#124016)

Engage the Brain: How to Design for Learning That Taps into the Power of Emotion by Allison Posey (#119015)

From Behaving to Belonging: The Inclusive Art of Supporting Students Who Challenge Us by Julie Causton & Kate MacLeod (#121011)

Learning to Choose, Choosing to Learn: The Key to Student Motivation and Achievement by Mike Anderson (#116015)

Learning That Sticks: A Brain-Based Model for K–12 Instructional Design and Delivery by Bryan Goodwin with Tonia Gibson & Kristin Rouleau (#120032)

The Power of the Adolescent Brain: Strategies for Teaching Middle and High School Students by Thomas Armstrong (#116017)

Research-Based Strategies to Ignite Student Learning: Insights from Neuroscience and the Classroom, Revised and Expanded Edition, by Judy Willis & Malana Willis (#120029)

Solving Academic and Behavior Problems: A Strengths-Based Guide for Teachers and Teams by Margaret Searle & Marilyn Swartz (#120016)

Teaching Students to Drive Their Brains: Metacognitive Strategies, Activities, and Lesson Ideas by Donna Wilson & Marcus Conyers (#117002)

Total Participation Techniques: Making Every Student an Active Learner, 2nd Edition, by Pérsida Himmele & William Himmele (#117033)

Why Are We Still Doing That? Positive Alternatives to Problematic Teaching Practices by Pérsida Himmele & William Himmele (#122010)

For up-to-date information about ASCD resources, go to www.ascd.org. You can search the complete archives of *Educational Leadership* at www.ascd.org/el. To contact us, send an email to member@ascd.org or call 1-800-933-2723 or 703-578-9600.

WHOLE CHILD
TENETS

1 **HEALTHY**
Each student enters school healthy and learns about and practices a healthy lifestyle.

2 **SAFE**
Each student learns in an environment that is physically and emotionally safe for students and adults.

3 **ENGAGED**
Each student is actively engaged in learning and is connected to the school and broader community.

4 **SUPPORTED**
Each student has access to personalized learning and is supported by qualified, caring adults.

5 **CHALLENGED**
Each student is challenged academically and prepared for success in college or further study and for employment and participation in a global environment.

The ASCD Whole Child approach is an effort to transition from a focus on narrowly defined academic achievement to one that promotes the long-term development and success of all children. Through this approach, ASCD supports educators, families, community members, and policymakers as they move from a vision about educating the whole child to sustainable, collaborative actions.

Promoting Student Attention relates to the **safe** *tenet. For more about the ASCD Whole Child approach, visit* ***www.ascd.org/wholechild.***